New Orleans
KITCHENS

New Orleans Kitchens

Recipes from the Big Easy's Best Restaurants

Stacey Meyer and Troy A. Gilbert
Foreword by Emeril Lagasse

GIBBS SMITH
TO ENRICH AND INSPIRE HUMANKIND

Dedicated to the artists and chefs
of New Orleans who
made this book possible.

First Edition
12 11 10 09 08   5 4 3 2 1

Published by
Gibbs Smith, Publisher
P.O. Box 667
Layton, Utah 84041

1.800.835.4993 orders
www.gibbs-smith.com

Designed by Kurt Wahlner
Printed and bound in Hong Kong

Library of Congress Cataloging-in-Publication Data

Meyer, Stacey.
    New Orleans kitchens : recipes from the Big Easy's best restau-
rants / Stacey Meyer and Troy A. Gilbert ; foreword by Emeril
Lagasse. — 1st ed.
        p. cm.
    ISBN-13: 978-1-4236-1001-4
    ISBN-10: 1-4236- 1001-6
    1. Cookery, American—Louisiana style. 2. Cookery—
Louisiana—New Orleans. I. Gilbert, Troy A. II. Title.
    TX715.2.L68M48 2010
    641.59763'35—dc22

                                2008007981

Pages 2 & 3:
*Delta Queen at Sunset, by Karl Kratzberg,
courtesy A.G. Wagner Studio.*

Right:
*Small World #22, by Allison Stewart,
courtesy Arthur Roger Gallery.*

Contents

Acknowledgments

*N*ew Orleans Kitchens was such an exciting project. We had the opportunity to meet some of New Orleans' most creative and interesting people. We want to acknowledge a few people in particular for their behind-the-scenes support.

Stacey's mom, Mary Ann Meyer, for being a great supporter, for contributing recipes, for testing recipes, and for being there during all the craziness.

Stephen Domas for his editorial skills and for his support.

Alyson Peters for submitting recipes and testing recipes for me.

Ken Berke for his amazing photographs of the art work—we should have used some of his photos as well.

Anna Minges for helping gather all of the images from The Ogden Museum and all of her hard work. She is an amazing woman.

Rick Gruber, one of the most knowledgeable people we have met regarding Southern art.

Leslie Spillman from Soren Christensen, Christy Wood and Denise R. Berthiaume from LeMieux—remarkable effort, Jonathon Ferrara for Art Docs, and Donna Cavato for The Edible Schoolyard Gardens. Not to mention, all the artists, galleries, and chefs who participated in this book.

Foreword

By Emeril J. Lagasse III

When most people think of New Orleans, they think food, fun, and frivolity, with the madness of Mardi Gras and Bourbon Street coming to mind first and foremost. But when you take the time to scratch the surface even just a bit, however, or if your visit to this fair city enables you to linger a while and take in everything that the Big Easy has to offer, you quickly see that not only is there this fun and delicious element always simmering around town, but also so much more that is part of the fabric of everyday life here. What is it about this city that inspires the artist in all of us, whether chef, author, painter, or musician?

These are thoughts that I sometimes ponder, many years after New Orleans called to me to make my home here. Over the years I have fallen in love with the city in many different ways–and the love affair continues. When I first arrived here almost thirty years ago, it was the food that called me, but once here it was the people and the joyful way that New Orleanians live life that cemented the union. My craft as a cook grew more and more inspired as I learned some of the secrets of the bold, flavorful Creole and Cajun cooking. The architecture and pulse of the rich art scene in the Warehouse District was a natural home to my first restaurant venture, and the community embraced me much as I had their city. Years later, with much history behind us all, I still keep coming back to the beat of this incredible city, which truly feels like home to me in a way no other place ever has.

I invite you to take a stroll through the city with me–her tastes, her visions, her music, her inspirations and aspirations, by exploring the pages of *New Orleans Kitchens*. My good friend Stacey Meyer has knocked on many doors and has assembled some truly delicious recipes and gems of the local art scene to share a little bit of the magic of the city with us all.

Come see a bit of what the Crescent City is all about . . .

Untitled Ships on River, *by Will Henry Stevens, courtesy Blue Spiral Gallery, and the Ogden Museum of Southern Art.*

Introduction

New Orleans is known as "The Crescent City." Shaped like a crescent and nestled on the banks of the Mississippi River, it was originally settled by the Spanish and French, and their influence is still reflected today in its culture, cuisine, and architecture. Throughout the nineteenth and twentieth centuries, people from France, Italy, Ireland and Germany, and more recently Vietnam, emigrated to the city, each bringing with them their unique heritage and traditions. In many ways, New Orleans is the melting pot of the South. It is a city that has a rich history and its diversity is reflected in its music, cuisine, arts, and architecture. As a port city, people of all walks of life flowed in and out of the community. Historically, the South was mainly rural with just a few cosmopolitan cities. New Orleans, Charleston and Savannah were the centers for arts and culture, but New Orleans had more of a Bohemian quality. New Orleans has always been considered the true southern mecca for musicians, writers, and artists. Its sultry and romantic atmosphere beckons quirky characters drawn to its allures. Artists draw inspiration from its landscape, architecture and people, while chefs draw inspiration from its unique and diverse cuisine and natural bounty of seafood or produce. Artists, musicians, writers, and chefs are all stimulated by the sense of community in New Orleans and are inspired by each other.

Southerners and Northerners alike flock to New Orleans for its music festivals; the Jazz and Heritage Festival being the main draw. Music is an inherent part of the city's soul with its gospel brunches and jazz funerals. In the spring, just before Mardi Gras, you can hear the high school brass bands practicing before performing in the parades. Walking through the French Quarter, trumpets and saxophones resonate in the street. New Orleans is famous for jazz and blues, but all forms of music can be found emanating from its many clubs and bars. There are endless venues for music, including such iconic establishments as Tipitina's and the Maple Leaf. Like everything else in New Orleans, its music has its own unique style and rhythm.

The cuisine of New Orleans is unlike anywhere else in the world. It is deeply rooted in the diverse heritage of the city. Jambalaya, for example, is a rice dish made with shrimp, chicken, and sausage, reminiscent of its Spanish culinary cousin paella. While gumbo is heavily influenced by the city's West African heritage, other famous dishes such as beignets and Trout Meunière Amandine come from France. With so many cultures converging in one spot, it is no wonder the food is as diverse and unique as it is delectable. Another key factor to the city's famous foods is the resources New Orleans and southern Louisiana have available. The Gulf of Mexico provides shrimp, blue crabs, and an endless list of fish. Louisiana cultivates more oysters than anywhere else in the country. The more exotic ingredients like alligator, crawfish, and frog's legs are also cultivated throughout southern Louisiana. This state is also known as "sportsman's paradise," where hunting and fishing are not just sports, but ways of life passed down through generations. There are innumerable cookbooks published in Louisiana dedicated to wild game that provide recipes for ducks, doves, venison, rabbits, squirrel, and possum. Fruit trees are grown in gardens and backyards throughout New Orleans. Pecan trees grow throughout the state, and rice and sugar cane are agricultural staples.

Louisiana natives love these heritage foods and the chefs of New Orleans prominently showcase them in their restaurants. New Orleanians love to eat, cook, and talk about food. It is an integral part of the city's culture.

Food in New Orleans, though based in tradition, has grown, expanded and evolved. It was once thought there were only five dishes in New Orleans: gumbo, crawfish étouffée, jambalaya, red beans and rice, and po' boys. Chefs, such as Paul Prudhomme, brought national attention to Cajun food and Emeril Lagasse wowed the nation with his exuberance and love for New Orleans and its cuisine. New Orleans has always had its stalwart restaurants. Galatoire's, Arnaud's, Brennan's, and Commanders Palace still serve the traditional dishes in grand style. As new chefs come to New Orleans from across the country and the world, they bring with them creative twists on old ideas. These talented new chefs are creating a fresh New Orleans cuisine that is innovative and exciting. Chefs like John Besh, Scott Boswell, and Allison and Slade Rushing are setting new standards with their bright style and creative menus.

After Hurricane Katrina devastated large swaths of the city in 2005, there was some worry that restaurants would have a hard time re-opening due to a lack of demand and staffing issues. While there were difficulties to overcome, New Orleans actually has more restaurants now than ever before. More boutique-style eateries have opened throughout town. Historically, if you wanted a sandwich, you were limited to a traditional po' boy, but with the opening of such eateries as St. James Cheese Shop and Stein's Market and Deli, you can enjoy more cheese-centric salads and sandwiches, as well as New York–style deli sandwiches. Parisian-style pastry shops such as Sucre, and Italian-style gelaterias have opened post-Katrina and offer their patrons delectable treats. There has also been an influx of Mexican and Central Americans to the city since Katrina, bringing with them their own traditional culinary styles and dishes. New Orleans is not just gumbo and po' boys any more.

One aspect of New Orleans culture that is often overlooked is its amazing art scene. For a small city, there is a huge art community. New Orleans draws artists from all over the world. Traditionally, most of the art galleries were located in the French Quarter where artists lived and worked. As the art community grew, galleries began popping up in other neighborhoods, such as the Warehouse District. Also known as the Arts District, the Warehouse District was home to the 1984 World's Fair. Though not a huge financial success for the city, the fair brought attention and helped to revitalize and preserve this historic neighborhood. A huge proponent for this urban renewal was chef Emeril Lagasse who opened his flagship restaurant in the heart of the district. Emeril was an urban pioneer and encouraged people to follow his lead. The old buildings and warehouses proved to be a perfect setting for showing and storing art. As more restaurants and galleries opened, the old warehouses were turned into New York–style lofts. Julia Street, at the heart of the Arts District, is home to more than twenty-five art galleries. The Contemporary Arts Center is located just a few blocks away, housed in an old pharmaceutical warehouse. In 2003, the Ogden Museum of

Southern Art opened just across the street. The Ogden Museum houses an extensive collection of art from around the South. The museum was the culmination of the vision of Roger Houston Ogden, an avid collector of Southern art. As his collection grew, so did his desire to make it available to the public. Mr. Ogden was an advocate of bringing recognition to Southern art and architecture, and was just as dedicated to the education of the rest of the nation. The Ogden Museum is quite a modern structure, made of smooth stone and expansive walls of glass. It sits directly next to the 1889 Patrick F. Taylor Library. The library is the only structure of its kind in the South designed by Louisiana native H. H. Richardson. The library is scheduled to reopen after renovation and will house eighteenth and nineteenth century works.

The contemporary building, known as Stephen Goldring Hall, appropriately houses the more modern works and The Ogden Museum is an example of an institution adding panache to this still up and coming neighborhood.

The juxtaposition of old and new signifies the evolution of not just the art and culinary community of New Orleans, but of New Orleans itself. More so than ever, New Orleans is striving for a harmonious balance of tradition and modern, progressive and historic; and nowhere is that more evident than in its art and cuisine. *New Orleans Kitchens* represents the traditional art and food of New Orleans, and showcases its ever evolving contemporary manifestations.

Appetizers

WHITE TRUFFLE BEAN DIP

Recipe courtesy of Tom Wolfe from Peristyle.

3 tablespoons Plugra butter
1 carrot
1 onion, halved
1 stalk celery
1 bay leaf
3/4 teaspoon chopped garlic
2 sprigs fresh thyme
1 pound white beans, rinsed and
   picked through
1 1/2 quarts vegetable stock
2 teaspoons salt
1 teaspoon freshly ground black pepper
1 tablespoon Creole mustard
1 tablespoon lemon juice
   White truffle oil to taste

In a 4-quart saucepot, melt the butter until bubbly; add the carrot, onion, celery, and bay leaf and sautée until tender but not brown. Add the garlic, thyme, white beans, vegetable stock, salt, and pepper. Bring to a boil then turn the heat down and allow the beans to simmer for 45 minutes to 1 hour. The beans should be slightly overcooked. Allow the beans to cool slightly and then remove the carrot, onion, celery, bay leaf, and thyme. Purée the beans in a blender until smooth. Pass the purée through a fine sieve. Add the Creole mustard, lemon juice, and white truffle oil. Serve with toasted bread or crackers.

Serves 4 to 6

Blue Sapphire, *by James Michalopoulos, courtesy Michalopoulos Gallery.*

CREOLE TOMATO BRUSCHETTA

Recipe courtesy of Scott Snodgrass from One.

4 ripe Creole or heirloom tomatoes, seeded and diced*
1 teaspoon chopped garlic
1 tablespoon chopped parsley
1/4 cup basil, chiffonade
1 tablespoon honey
2 tablespoons balsamic vinegar
2 tablespoons extra virgin olive oil
1 to 2 teaspoons kosher salt
Freshly ground black pepper to taste

Combine all ingredients in a large bowl and mix thoroughly. Serve with toast points or your favorite crackers.

Serves 6

---

* Any ripe tomato may be substituted.

Garlic, by Billy Solitario, courtesy LeMieux Galleries.

Oak, by Kate Trepagnier, courtesy LeMieux Galleries.

MARINATED KALAMATA OLIVES

Recipe courtesy of Tom Wolfe from Peristyle.

2   cups kalamata olives, pitted and drained
2   shallots, minced
1   teaspoon chopped thyme
2   teaspoons chopped basil
1   teaspoon chopped oregano
1   teaspoon chopped Italian parsley
1/2 teaspoon chopped rosemary
1   teaspoon chopped garlic
    Juice of 2 lemons
1/3 cup extra virgin olive oil
    Freshly ground black pepper

Combine all ingredients in a large bowl and marinate for at least 2 hours before serving. Serve with toothpicks.

Serves 6 to 8

CRAB PHYLLO TRIANGLES

Recipe courtesy of Mary Ann Meyer.

1 3/4 cups unsalted butter, divided
1 bunch scallions, minced
1 clove garlic, minced
1 small yellow onion, diced small
8 ounces cream cheese, softened
1 pound lump crabmeat, cleaned
2 eggs, slightly beaten
2 teaspoons lemon juice
1 teaspoon Tabasco sauce
1 package phyllo dough, defrosted

Preheat oven to 375 degrees.

In a medium sautée pan, melt $1/4$ cup butter over low heat. Add the scallions, garlic, and onion and sautée until translucent, about 3 minutes. Add the cream cheese, stirring until completely melted. Add crabmeat, eggs, lemon juice, and Tabasco sauce. Stir until all ingredients are well incorporated.

Melt the remaining butter in a small saucepan or in the microwave. Cut the phyllo dough into 3-inch-wide strips. Use 1 strip at a time, keeping other strips covered with a damp cloth until ready to use. Brush 1 strip of dough with melted butter. Place 1 tablespoon crabmeat mixture on one end of the strip. Fold one edge of the dough over mixture to form a triangle; continue folding like you would fold a flag. Place the triangle on a baking sheet and brush with a little melted butter. Repeat this process until all of the filling has been used. Any leftover phyllo dough may be refrozen. Bake for 12 to 15 minutes.

Serves 6 to 8

Lawrence Street Market, *by Anton Haardt, courtesy Anton Haardt Gallery.*

Magazine Street Balcony, 1998, by Amy McKinnon, courtesy Amy McKinnon.

MINI CRAWFISH PIES

Recipe courtesy of Stacey Meyer.

1/4   cup canola oil
3/4   cup flour
1/2   cup minced green bell pepper
1/3   cup minced yellow onion
1 1/2 cups heavy cream
3/4   cup butter
3/4   cup thinly sliced scallions
2   cloves garlic, minced
1 1/2 pounds Louisiana crawfish tails,
       roughly chopped
1   tablespoon salt
3/4   teaspoon red pepper flakes
3/4   teaspoon black pepper
1   teaspoon filé powder
1/4   teaspoon dried thyme
1/4   teaspoon dried basil
1/4   teaspoon Paul Prudhomme's
       Seafood Seasoning
24   mini tart shells (2-inch diameter)

Preheat oven to 400 degrees.

In a large saucepan over medium heat, add oil; when hot, add flour and make a dark roux, stirring constantly so it does not burn. When the roux is dark brown, add the bell pepper and onion. Cook for about 3 minutes to just sweat the vegetables. Add the cream and bring to a simmer.

In a separate pan, melt butter over medium heat; add the scallions, garlic, and crawfish and then cook for 3 to 5 minutes. Add all the seasonings and combine the crawfish with the cream mixture; simmer another 20 to 25 minutes. Fill the tart shells with about 2 tablespoons of the crawfish mixture. Bake for 15 minutes, or until the shells are fully cooked. Serve warm.

Yields 24 mini pies

WARM CRABMEAT DIP

Recipe courtesy of Mary Ann Meyer.

1/2 cup butter
1/2 cup minced scallions
1/4 cup chopped parsley
  2 tablespoons flour
  2 cups whole milk
  8 ounces cream cheese
  1 pound lump crabmeat, cleaned
  1 teaspoon Tabasco sauce
1/2 teaspoon salt
1/2 teaspoon freshly ground white pepper

In a medium saucepan, melt butter over medium-low heat. When butter begins to bubble, add scallions and parsley; cook for 3 minutes, or until scallions are translucent. Add flour and stir to coat vegetables; add milk and cook for 5 minutes. Add cream cheese and stir until blended. Add crabmeat and seasonings, stirring well; cook over low heat until the crabmeat is hot. Serve in a chaffing dish with warm bread, or serve individually on slices of toasted baguette.

Serves 6 to 8

Empty Silence, by Rolland Golden, *courtesy Rolland Golden.*

Gulf Waters, *by Dean Mitchell, courtesy Bryant Galleries.*

LOUISIANA OYSTERS AND TEQUILA LIME GRANITA

Recipe courtesy of Chuck Subra from La Côte Brasserie.

- 1/2 cup plus 1 tablespoon fresh lime juice
- 1/4 cup plus 2 tablespoons rice wine vinegar
- 1/4 cup tequila
- 2 tablespoons sugar
  Salt and freshly ground black pepper
    to taste
- 24 Louisiana oysters on the half shell

In a small bowl, combine the lime juice, rice wine vinegar, tequila, and sugar. Whisk these ingredients together and season to taste with salt and pepper. Pour liquid into a baking dish and place in the freezer over night. Occasionally, stir the mixture.

Serve the oysters on the half shell. Remove the granita from the freezer and, using a spoon, shave the ice. Place 1 teaspoon of the granita on each oyster. Serve chilled.

Serves 4 to 6

Three Dune Crowns, by Billy Solitario, courtesy LeMieux Galleries.

MAHI MAHI CEVICHE

Recipe courtesy of Alyson Peters.

1 pint grape tomatoes, halved
2 cucumbers, seeded and quartered
1 red bell pepper, diced small
1 Vidalia onion, diced small
3 pounds mahi mahi, cut into 1/2-inch cubes
6 limes, juiced
2 naval oranges, juiced
1/2 cup chopped cilantro
2 tablespoons olive oil
    Salt and pepper to taste
    Mixed greens
1 ripe avocado, diced

Combine all of the ingredients except for the mixed greens and avocado and refrigerate for 24 hours. Serve mixture on a bed of mixed greens with the avocado sprinkled over top.

Serves 6 to 8

Live Oaks and Fountain, by Bobby Wozniak, courtesy LeMieux Galleries.

Blue Grey Fish, *by Archie Bonge, courtesy Bonge Foundation and the Ogden Museum of Southern Art.*

TUNA POKE

Recipe courtesy of Chuck Subra from La Côte Brasserie.

2 pounds raw tuna loin
3 tablespoons sesame oil
3 tablespoons soy sauce
1 teaspoon grated fresh ginger
2 tablespoons hot sauce
4 ounces seaweed salad*
  Sea salt
1 English cucumber

* Seaweed salad is a premade mix and can be purchased at Asian markets, from your local sushi restaurant, or at Whole Foods health food markets.

Dice raw tuna into $1/4$- to $1/2$-inch pieces. In a small bowl, combine sesame oil, soy sauce, ginger, and hot sauce. Whisk well and then fold in diced tuna and seaweed salad; season with sea salt and let marinate for 5 to 10 minutes.

Slice the English cucumber into $1/8$-inch rounds. Top each cucumber slice with 2 teaspoons of the marinated tuna and serve immediately.

Serves 6 to 8

Red Coin du Lestin, *by George Dunbar, courtesy Ogden Museum of Southern Art.*

OYSTERS ROCKEFELLER

Recipe courtesy of Brian Landry, Executive Chef Galatoire's Restaurant, from Galatoire's: Biography of a Bistro, *by Marda Burton and Kenneth Holditch (Hill Street Press).*

3/4 cup chopped fennel
    (bulb only)
1/4 cup chopped leeks
    (green and white parts)
1/4 cup finely chopped
    curly parsley
1/4 cup finely chopped
    green onions, green
    and white parts
1/4 cup chopped celery
1/4 cup ketchup
1 1/2 cups cooked and drained
    chopped frozen spinach
1/2 teaspoon salt
1/2 teaspoon freshly ground
    white pepper
1/2 teaspoon cayenne pepper
1 teaspoon dried thyme leaves
1 teaspoon ground anise
2 teaspoons Worcestershire
    sauce
1/4 cup Herbsaint liqueur
1 cup melted butter
1/2 cup seasoned dried
    breadcrumbs
12 cups rock salt
6 dozen oysters on the
    half shell
12 lemon wedges

Preheat the oven to 350 degrees.

In a food processor, combine the fennel, leeks, parsley, green onions, celery, ketchup, spinach, salt, white pepper, cayenne pepper, thyme, anise, Worcestershire, and Herbsaint. Purée the mixture thoroughly. Using a rubber spatula, scrape the contents of the food processor into a large mixing bowl. Stir in the butter and the breadcrumbs, making sure the mixture is well blended.

Pour enough rock salt into twelve 8-inch cake pans to cover the bottoms of pans. Arrange 6 oysters in their half shells in each pan.

Fill a pastry bag with the purée and pipe the sauce over each oyster. Or use a tablespoon to distribute the sauce.

Place the pans in the oven and bake for 5 minutes, or until the sauce sets. Turn the heat up to broil and broil the oysters for 3 to 4 minutes, or until the tops are bubbling. It may be necessary to bake the oysters in batches.

Line each plate with cloth napkins that have been folded into neat squares. Nestle the pans of oysters within the folded napkins. Garnish with lemon wedges and serve at once.

Serves 12

Galatoire's, by Fredrick Guess, courtesy Fredrick Guess Studios.

STEAMED COCKSCOMB GINGER CRAWFISH DUMPLINGS

Recipe courtesy of Matt Guidry from Meauxbar.

DUMPLING FILLING

- 3 tablespoons canola oil
- 1/4 cup minced garlic
- 1/4 cup minced fresh ginger
- 1 pound crawfish tail meat (preferably Louisiana), drained and coarsely chopped
- 3/4 teaspoon nuoc nam (fish sauce)
- 1/4 cup oyster sauce
- 1 tablespoon sambal oelek
- Pinch of sugar
- 1/2 cup chopped cilantro leaves
- 1/2 cup chopped green onion, tops only
- 1 tablespoon sesame oil
- 1 package square or round wonton wrappers
- 1 egg beaten with 1 tablespoon water

SESAME SOY DIPPING SAUCE

- 1/4 cup rice vinegar
- 1 tablespoon sesame oil
- 1 tablespoon minced green onion, tops only
- 1/2 cup soy sauce
- Pinch of sugar

In a medium sautée pan, place the canola oil over high heat; cook the garlic and ginger until golden. Add crawfish tail meat, fish sauce, oyster sauce, sambal oelek, and sugar. Cook 1 minute to remove excess moisture. Add cilantro, green onions, and sesame oil, stirring well to combine; remove from heat. Spread filling mixture onto a sheet pan, allowing any excess moisture to escape; cool thoroughly.

Place a wonton wrapper on a work surface and spoon in 1 tablespoon of the filling. Brush wrapper edges with egg wash and fold in half to form a semicircle. Pinch edges together to seal and make pleats. Alternately, place a wonton wrapper in a Gow Gee Press* and put the filling in the center. Brush edges of wrapper with egg wash and close press firmly to seal edges. Steam dumplings for 4 minutes and serve immediately with the Sesame Soy Dipping Sauce.

To make the dipping sauce, combine all ingredients together and mix well.

Serves 8 and yields 40 dumplings

---

* A Gow Gee Press can be purchased at the World Market. This press is not necessary, it just makes it easier.

French Quarter Roses Study, *by John Preble, courtesy John Preble.*

Bloody Mary Shrimp and Pickled Mirliton Ceviche

Recipe courtesy of Chuck Subra from Côte Brasserie.

1 tablespoon vegetable oil
5 pounds Louisiana shrimp (peeled)
6 ounces vodka
2 mirliton, diced small
   (also known as chayote)
1 red onion, diced small
2 limes, juiced
1 tablespoon Worcestershire sauce
1 tablespoon Tabasco sauce
1 bottle (32 ounces) Bloody
   Mary Mix
   Sea salt and black pepper

In a medium sautée pan over high heat, add vegetable oil and then heat the shrimp and cook thoroughly; remove from heat and chill.

In a medium mixing bowl, combine the chilled shrimp, vodka, mirliton, onion, lime juice, Worcestershire sauce, Tabasco, and Bloody Mary Mix. Season to taste with sea salt and black pepper and then refrigerate over night.

Serves 8

Ham Fish, *by Francie Rich, courtesy Francie Rich.*

PEPPADEW POPPERS

Recipe courtesy of Bob Iacaovone from Cuvee.

10 peppadew peppers*
3 ounces goat cheese
10 slices serrano ham or prosciutto, thinly sliced

---

* Peppadew peppers are pickled peppers from South Africa. They are sold in a jar or in the olive bar section of your grocery store. They are about the size of cherry tomatoes, bright red, sour, sweet, and spicy. They can also be found at gourmet markets or online.

Preheat oven to 350 degrees.

Stuff each pepper with some goat cheese and then wrap each with prosciutto. Bake in the oven until crisp, about 3 to 4 minutes. Serve warm.

Serves 4

Architect Dreams #1,
by Nicole Charbonnet,
courtesy Arthur Roger Gallery.

Char-Grilled Oysters with Roquefort Cheese and Red Wine Vinaigrette

Recipe courtesy of Scott Snodgrass from One.

2	bunches scallions, sliced
1	tablespoon chopped garlic
1	tablespoon chopped shallot
1/8	cup honey
1	cup red wine vinegar
1	cup olive oil
2	cups crumbled Roquefort cheese
2	lemons, juiced
2	tablespoons kosher salt
1/2	tablespoon crushed red pepper flakes
3	dozen oysters on the half shell

In a large bowl, mix together all the ingredients except the oysters, trying not to break up the cheese too much; set aside.

Prepare a hot grill. Charcoal is preferred, but a gas grill is fine as long as it is hot. When grill is hot, place oysters in the half shell directly on the grill and ladle 2 tablespoons of the vinaigrette on each oyster. Grill for about 3 to 4 minutes, or until the oysters plump up and their edges begin to curl. Serve immediately.

Serves 6

Fairway Grocery, *by Shirley Rabe Masinter, courtesy LeMieux Galleries.*

NEW ORLEANS FERMENTED BLACK BEAN BBQ SHRIMP

Recipe courtesy of Steve Schwarz of Mat and Naddies.

4 ounces or 1/4 cup fermented black beans*
1 tablespoon sesame oil
2 tablespoons minced ginger
2 tablespoons minced garlic
1/4 cup sliced scallions
1/4 cup minced shallot
1 lemon, zested and juiced
1/2 cup Worcestershire sauce
2 tablespoons brown sugar
1 1/2 teaspoons black pepper
1 1/2 teaspoons sambal oelek
1/2 cup ketchup
1 tablespoon sesame oil
1/4 cup vegetable oil, divided
2 pounds large shrimp, head on
1/2 pound butter

* Can be purchased in Asian markets. Prepared black bean sauce, such as Lee Kum Kee brand, can be substituted. It can be found in the Asian section of many grocery stores.

Rinse black beans to remove salt and drain.

In a medium sautée pan over medium heat, add the sesame oil; sweat the ginger, garlic, scallions, shallot, and lemon zest until very soft, about 3 to 4 minutes. Deglaze the pan with the lemon juice and Worcestershire sauce; add the and brown sugar. Season with black pepper and sambal (more may be added than called for depending on the amount of heat desired). Add the ketchup and sesame oil and cook for 10 to 15 minutes.

In a heavy cast-iron skillet, heat half of the vegetable oil and add about half of the shrimp to the pan. When the shrimp start to turn pink, add about one-half of the black bean sauce and continue to cook until the shrimp are almost done. Add the butter and stir continuously while butter melts. You may need to add a little water if the sauce gets too thick. Continue cooking the shrimp in batches with the remaining oil until all have been cooked. Serve with Jasmine rice and Chinese vegetables.

Serves 4

Dixie Shadows, *by Gretchen Wheaton, courtesy LeMieux Galleries.*

Beverages

CREOLE TOMATO BLOODY MARY (HANGOVER CURE ALL)

Recipe courtesy of Chuck Subra from La Côte Brasserie.

1	Creole or other tomato
2	ounces vodka
4	ounces V8 juice
1	teaspoon A1 Steak Sauce
1/8	teaspoon horseradish
1	dash freshly ground black pepper
1	dash celery salt
1	dash Tabasco sauce
	Crushed ice
1	pickled green bean (optional)

In a pint glass, muddle or crush the tomato. Add the vodka, V8, steak sauce, horseradish, black pepper, celery salt, and Tabasco. Add crushed ice and garnish with the pickled green bean.

Serves 1

HUCKLEBERRY MOJITO

Recipe courtesy of Scott Snodgrass from One.

1	stem mint with leaves
1	heaping tablespoon huckleberries or blueberries
1/2	lime, juiced
2	ounces simple syrup
	Crushed ice
2 to 3	ounces light rum
	Club soda

Tear mint leaves and stem into little pieces. Place leaves, stem, berries, lime juice, and simple syrup into a rocks glass and then muddle or crush for 20 to 30 seconds. Pour mixture into an 8-ounce tumbler and then top with crushed ice. Add the rum and then top with soda. Garnish with any extra mint leaves and a few berries.

Serves 1

Untitled Work on Paper, *by Dusti Bonge, courtesy Bonge Foundation.*

Ruston Peach Fuzzy Naval Martini

Recipe courtesy of Chuck Subra from La Côte Brasserie.

1   Ruston peach or any other peach
1 1/2 ounces peach schnapps
1 1/2 ounces triple sec
1 1/2 ounces orange juice
    Crushed ice

Remove pit and skin from peach and then purée peach in a blender. In a shaker, combine the peach purée, schnapps, triple sec, orange juice, and ice. Shake well for 30 seconds and strain into martini glasses.

Serves 4

Planter's Punch

Recipe courtesy of Stacey Meyer.

1 1/2 ounces gold rum
1 1/2 ounces light rum
1   ounce lime juice
1   ounce lemon juice
1   dash grenadine
1   dash Herbsaint liqueur
1   scoop crushed ice
    Lemon-lime soda
1   lemon slice, seeded

Mix all ingredients, except the soda and the lemon slice, in a shaker or a blender. Pour into a chilled highball glass and top with cold soda. Garnish with lemon slice.

Serves 1

Gede, by Roy Ferdinand, courtesy Anton Haardt Gallery.

KUMQUAT COSMO

Recipe courtesy of Chuck Subra from La Côte Brasserie.

2 kumquats
1 1/2 ounces pomegranate vodka
1/2 ounce triple sec
1 1/2 ounces cranberry juice
1/2 ounce fresh-squeezed
    lime juice
    Crushed ice

Remove seeds from the kumquat and then muddle or crush the kumquat for 30 seconds. Add the vodka, triple sec, cranberry juice, and lime juice. Add ice and shake in a shaker until well mixed. Strain into a martini glass. Garnish with a kumquat round, if desired.

Serves 1

PINEAPPLE RUM SODA

Recipe courtesy of Alyson Peters.

2 to 3 ounces Mount Gay rum
1 ounce pineapple juice
1 ounce lime juice
    Crushed ice
    Soda water
1 lime wedge

In a shaker, combine the rum, pineapple juice, lime juice, and some crushed ice. Strain into a highball glass filled with crushed ice and garnish with a lime wedge.

Serves 1

Bowl of Shells, *by Benjamin Shamback, courtesy LeMieux Galleries.*

BRANDY MILK PUNCH

Recipe courtesy of Stacey Meyer.

2 ounces brandy
1 ounce crème de cacao
3/4 cup milk
1/4 teaspoon vanilla extract
1 teaspoon powdered sugar
1 scoop crushed ice
  Nutmeg and cinnamon to taste

Combine all of the ingredients except for the nutmeg and cinnamon in a shaker. Mix well and serve in a cocktail glass. Garnish with a dash each of cinnamon and nutmeg.

Serves 1

MARIE LAVEAUX

Recipe courtesy of Stacey Meyer.

3/4 ounce dark rum
3/4 ounce brandy
1/4 ounce Frangelico
1/4 ounce Kahlúa
1 cup cold brewed coffee
2 teaspoons brown sugar
2 tablespoons heavy cream
2 scoops crushed ice

Combine all ingredients in a shaker or a blender and mix well. Pour into cocktail glasses and serve.

Serves 2

MANGO MOJITO

Recipe courtesy of Stacey Meyer.

1/2 lime, juiced
1 teaspoon superfine sugar
   Mint leaves to taste, plus one or
     two for garnish
1 tablespoon mango purée
1 scoop crushed ice
2 ounces light rum
   Soda water

Place lime juice and sugar in a glass; stir to dissolve sugar. Add a few mint leaves and then muddle or crush in the glass. Add the mango purée. Fill the glass with crushed ice and then pour in the rum. Top off with the soda water and garnish with mint.

Serves 1

PONCHATOULA STRAWBERRY SANGRIA

Recipe courtesy of Chuck Subra from La Côte Brasserie.

2 pints Ponchatoula or other strawberries,
   stemmed and cut in half
1/4 cup sugar
1 Louisiana naval orange, peeled
1/2 bottle or 2 cups red wine (good quality)
1 cup orange juice
2 cups lemon-lime soda

Wash and remove the stems and hulls from the strawberries. In a pitcher, add the strawberries, sugar, and orange slices; muddle or crush for 30 seconds. Add the red wine, orange juice, and soda. Mix well and then place in the refrigerator overnight. Serve the following day over ice. Garnish with slices of strawberry, if desired.

Serves 4

Spirit Returns, *by Rolland Golden, courtesy Rolland Golden.*

WASHINGTON PARISH WATERMELON

Recipe courtesy of Chuck Subra from La Côte Brasserie.

8   ounces Washington Parish or other
    watermelon, seeded
3   ounces vodka
1   ounce Southern Comfort
1   ounce Midori
1   ounce fresh orange juice
1/4 ounce pineapple juice
1   ounce grenadine

In a pitcher, add the watermelon and muddle or crush for 30 seconds. Add the vodka, Southern Comfort, Midori, orange juice, pineapple juice, and grenadine. Mix thoroughly and then fill pitcher with ice. Strain and serve over ice.

Serves 4

SATSUMA MOJITO

Recipe courtesy of Chuck Subra from La Côte Brasserie.

8   mint leaves
1   satsuma orange or tangerine, peeled
    and seeded
4   tablespoons light brown Louisiana sugar
3   ounces light rum
1/2 ounce lime juice
1   ounce lemon juice
1   cup crushed ice
    Lemon-lime soda
    Sugar cane sticks
    Lime wedges

In a rocks glass, combine the mint, orange slices, and brown sugar; muddle or crush for 30 seconds. Add the rum, lime juice, lemon juice, and crushed ice. Pour into a shaker and mix well. Strain into a rocks glass with ice. Top with soda and garnish with sugar cane sticks and lime wedges.

Serves 4

WATERMELON LIME SPRITZER

Recipe courtesy of Stacey Meyer.

1 1/2 cups cubed watermelon, seeded
3 tablespoons lime juice
1 teaspoon superfine sugar
1 scoop crushed ice
Soda water
1 lime wedge, seeded

Combine all ingredients except the soda water and lime wedge in a blender. Pour into a highball glass and top with soda. Garnish with lime wedge.

Serves 1

MANGO FREEZE

Recipe courtesy of Stacey Meyer.

1 ripe mango
3/4 cup mango juice
1 tablespoon honey
1 tablespoon lime juice
2 scoops crushed ice

Combine all ingredients in a blender and then serve immediately.

Serves 2

Clementine Going to Kitchen, *by Clementine Hunter,*
courtesy Ogden Museum of Southern Art.

BLUEBERRY LEMONADE

Recipe courtesy of Stacey Meyer.

3 cups blueberries
3/4 cup sugar
2 cups fresh-squeezed lemon juice
3 cups water
  Crushed ice
1/2 cup mint leaves, to garnish

Combine the blueberries and sugar in a blender and purée until smooth. Strain the blueberries through a fine mesh sieve. Combine the lemon juice and water. Add the blueberry purée to the lemon juice and water. Fill glasses with ice, and then pour mixture over top. Garnish each glass with mint and serve immediately.

Serves 4

PONCHATOULA STRAWBERRY LEMONADE

Recipe courtesy of Stacey Meyer.

3 cups sliced Ponchatoula or other
  strawberries
3/4 cup sugar
2 cups fresh-squeezed lemon juice
3 cups water
1/4 cup basil leaves, roughly torn, to garnish
  Crushed ice

Combine the strawberries and sugar in a blender and purée until smooth. Strain the strawberries through a fine mesh sieve. Combine the lemon juice and water. Add the strawberry purée to the lemon juice and water. Fill glasses with ice, and then pour mixture over top. Garnish each glass with basil leaves and serve immediately.

Serves 4

Blue Pitcher on Aluminum, *by Benjamin Shamback, courtesy LeMieux Galleries.*

Brunch

CRAB AND CORN FRITTERS

Recipe courtesy of Greg Sonnier.

1/2 cup all-purpose flour
1 cup yellow corn flour*
1 teaspoon baking powder
2 eggs
1/4 cup milk (more if needed)
1/2 cup finely diced red bell peppers
1/4 cup sliced green onions
1 cup freshly cut corn (with milk from the cobs)
1 teaspoon seafood seasoning
1/2 pound fresh lump crabmeat
2 sticks butter

---

* Corn flour comes from maize; it is much finer than cornmeal and acts as a thickener, and is often used in baking. It can be found in Latin markets or the Latin aisle at the grocery store. King Arthur or Bob's Red Mill brands can be found in health food stores and online.

Mix flour, corn flour, and baking powder together.

In a separate bowl, beat the eggs and milk together; stir in flour mixture. Add bell peppers, green onions, corn, and seasoning; stir well, then fold in crabmeat. (If mixture seems dry add a little more milk.)

To clarify the butter, place the butter in a small saucepan; melt slowly. Let stand for 1 to 2 minutes. Skim off the foam that rises to the top and gently pour the butter off the milk solids that have settled to the bottom.

In a skillet over medium-high heat, fry dollops of crab mixture in the clarified butter, turning only once, until fritters are golden brown about 3 minutes.

Serves 4

Thining Marsh, Ycloskey, *by Bobby Wozniak, courtesy LeMieux Galleries.*

Untitled Kitchens and Dining Rooms, *by Robert Brantley, courtesy Robert Brantley.*

GULF SHRIMP AND STONE-GROUND GRITS WITH ANDOUILLE SAUSAGE RED-EYE GRAVY

Recipe courtesy of Emanuelle Loubier from Dante's Kitchen.

1/2 gallon whole milk
1 pound unsalted butter
2 cups stone-ground grits
    Salt and pepper to taste
3 links fresh andouille sausage
3 tablespoons vegetable oil, divided
1 onion, thinly sliced
2 cups chicken stock
1 large shot espresso
    Worcestershire and Tabasco sauces to taste
1 pound large shrimp, heads and tails left intact for presentation
    Creole seafood seasoning to coat
    Parsley, chopped

In a large saucepan, heat milk and butter together until butter is melted. Add grits, reduce heat, and cook for about 1 hour over very low heat, stirring often. Season with salt and pepper to taste.

In a separate pan, cook the sausage in 1 tablespoon vegetable oil until brown; add onion and cook until translucent. Add chicken stock, espresso, Worcestershire, and Tabasco and then simmer for 45 minutes.

Toss the shrimp in Creole seasoning and then cook in remaining vegetable oil or just throw them on the grill. Serve the shrimp and gravy over the grits. Garnish with chopped parsley.

Serves 4

LOUISIANA BLUE CRAB CAKES WITH MANGO ANCHO AND CHIPOTLE CHUTNEY

Recipe courtesy of Stephen G. Schwarz from Mat and Naddies.

CRAB CAKES

- 1/2 pouch saltine crackers, crushed and divided
- 1/4 cup mayonnaise
- 1 tablespoon yellow mustard
- 2 tablespoons Worcestershire sauce
- 1 egg, beaten
- 1 pound lump crabmeat, cleaned
- 1 teaspoon black pepper
- 1 teaspoon baking powder
- 1/2 cup minced parsley
- 1 scallion, minced using both green and white parts
- 1/2 cup finely diced red bell pepper
- 2 tablespoons Seafood Boil Seasoning (see right)
- 1 lemon, juiced and zested
- 1/4 pound clarified butter (see page 59)
- 1 cup Mango Ancho and Chipotle Chutney (see right)

SEAFOOD BOIL SEASONING

- 1 tablespoon black pepper
- 6 bay leaves
- 1/2 teaspoon whole cardamom
- 1/2 teaspoon mustard seed
- 4 cloves
- 1 teaspoon paprika
- 1/4 teaspoon mace

MANGO ANCHO AND CHIPOTLE CHUTNEY

- 4 mangoes
- 1 tablespoon salt
- 5 dried ancho peppers
- 5 chipotle peppers
- 4 cloves garlic
- 1 ounce ginger
- 1/2 cup cider vinegar
- 2 tablespoons canola oil
- 2 teaspoons mustard seeds
- 1/2 cup brown sugar
- 1/4 teaspoon tumeric
- 3 tablespoons raisins
- 1 cup water

Scrub Oak Fighting The Wind, by Billy Solitario, courtesy LeMieux Galleries.

Put half the saltines in a pan or on a wide plate and reserve for dredging crab cakes.

In a medium-size bowl, combine mayonnaise, mustard, Worcestershire sauce, and egg. Gently fold in the crabmeat. Add black pepper, baking powder, parsley, scallion, bell pepper, Seafood Boil Seasoning, and lemon juice and zest; gently combine. Scoop $1/4$ cup of the crab mixture onto the plate of crushed saltines and coat evenly.

To make the Seafood Boil Seasoning, combine all ingredients in a spice grinder or small food processor. Grind well and store in a small glass jar.

In a cast-iron skillet over low heat, fry the crab cakes in the clarified butter. Serve with a dollop of the Mango Ancho and Chipotle Chutney.

To make the Mango Ancho and Chipotle Chutney, peel and dice the mangoes; salt them and then set aside.

De-stem and seed peppers. Soak in hot water until soft. Grind peppers, garlic, ginger, and vinegar in a blender to a smooth paste. Add a little water if necessary.

Heat oil in a saucepan and add the mustard seeds. When the seeds begin to pop, add the pepper mixture and fry while stirring. Add sugar and tumeric. Simmer for 10 minutes. Add mangoes, raisins, and water; simmer until slightly soft. Reduce heat and cook until thick.

Serves 4

CREPES DEGAS

Recipe courtesy of Ryan Hughes from Café Degas.

CREPES

- 2 eggs
- 1/3 cup flour
- 1/2 cup milk
- 2 tablespoons melted butter
- Pinch of salt

FILLING

- 2 tablespoons unsalted butter
- 1/2 pound wild mushrooms
- Salt and freshly ground pepper to taste
- 1 clove garlic, minced
- 2 tablespoons minced shallots
- 1 bunch asparagus, cooked and thinly sliced
- 1 pound jumbo lump crabmeat
- 1/4 cup brandy
- Cayenne pepper to taste
- 1 cup Hollandaise Sauce (see below)

HOLLANDAISE SAUCE

- 3 egg yolks
- 2 tablespoons lemon juice
- 1/4 teaspoon salt
- 1/2 cup melted butter
- Freshly ground white pepper

To make crepes, whisk or blend ingredients thoroughly. Allow to rest 30 minutes or as long as overnight. Whisk batter to thoroughly combine and remove any lumps. Lightly brush an 8-inch nonstick skillet with a teaspoon of butter and heat over medium heat. When the pan is hot, remove it from the heat and pour 1/4 cup batter into the pan. Swirl the pan to evenly coat the bottom. Return the pan to the heat and cook until lightly golden, about 30 seconds to 1 minute. Turn and cook on the other side for 30 seconds. Remove from the pan and place on a parchment-lined plate. Repeat with remaining batter, stacking the crepes with squares of parchment paper (or waxed paper) between each to prevent sticking. Any leftover crepes may be frozen in a ziplock bag for up to 2 weeks.

To make the filling, melt the butter in a medium sautée pan and cook mushrooms; season with salt and pepper. Add garlic and shallots and sweat for 2 minutes. Fold in asparagus and crabmeat and then flame with brandy; season with more salt and pepper and a touch of cayenne pepper. Wrap in crepe and serve warm with Hollandaise Sauce.

To make the sauce, add the egg yolks, lemon juice, and salt to a blender; blend on high for 30 seconds. While still blending, add the warm butter in a slow, steady stream until the sauce thickens. Season with pepper.

Serves 4

Chave and Chair, *by Gretchen Wheaton, courtesy LeMieux Galleries.*

Winky, *by John Preble, courtesy John Preble.*

LOUISIANA FROG'S LEGS "GRILLADES-STYLE," BACON AND CHEDDAR GRITS, AND POACHED EGGS

Recipe courtesy of Chef Greg Picolo from The Bistro at The Maison de Ville.

FROG'S LEGS

2 to 4 frog's legs per person, depending on size, seasoned with salt and pepper, and lightly dusted with all-purpose flour
3 tablespoons peanut oil
2 large onions, finely diced
2 stalks celery, finely diced
1 green bell pepper, finely diced
3 cups veal demi-glace or 9 cups beef stock, reduced to 3 cups
3 cloves garlic, minced
3 tablespoons lite soy sauce
1 tablespoon tamarind concentrate*
2 large ripe tomatoes, peeled, seeded and finely chopped
2 teaspoons minced parsley

BACON AND CHEDDAR GRITS

2 cups water
2 cups milk
2 cups uncooked grits
1 teaspoon salt
1 teaspoon white pepper
6 to 8 strips crispy, cooked bacon, crumbled
1 cup grated cheddar cheese

In a large sautée pan, cook legs briefly in hot oil until lightly browned. Remove legs from pan, drain two-thirds of the oil from the pan, and then return to heat and add onions, celery, and bell pepper. Sautée over medium heat for 5 to 10 minutes, and then add demi-glace or reduced stock, garlic, soy sauce, tamarind, tomatoes, and parsley. Let simmer over medium-low heat for 15 to 20 minutes, or until vegetables are cooked; season with salt and pepper to taste. Return legs to pan and cook an additional 10 minutes over low heat until medium rare. Don't overcook the legs as they may toughen.

To make the grits, heat the water and milk in a medium saucepan. When it comes to a boil add the grits and stir vigorously. Add salt and pepper and cook for 30 minutes, or until done. Add the bacon and cheese and stir until the cheese is melted; keep covered until ready to assemble dish.

Recipe continued on page 69

* Available in the Latin aisle of most grocery stores or at any Latin grocery store.

POACHED EGGS

2 eggs per person
water
rice vinegar

To assemble, poach 2 eggs per person by cracking the eggs into a simmering pot of six parts water to one part rice vinegar, until whites are set and yolks are warm, about 3 minutes. Place grits in the center of each plate, spoon frog's legs and sauce onto grits and top with poached eggs. Serve warm.

Serves 4 to 6

Dream Car, *by Jason Langley,*
courtesy Jason Langley.

LOUISIANA CRAWFISH AND MIRLITON BEIGNETS

Recipe courtesy of Chuck Subra from La Côte Brasserie.

1 pound Louisiana crawfish tail meat, roughly chopped
2 mirlitons, diced small (also known as chayotes)
1 teaspoon Tabasco sauce
2 Idaho potatoes, peeled, boiled and mashed
    Salt and pepper to taste
1 box (28 ounces) beignet mix
2 quarts cooking oil
1/4 cup powered sugar

In a mixing bowl, combine the crawfish, mirlitons, Tabasco, and potatoes. Mix thoroughly and season to taste with salt and pepper. Roll mixture into quarter-size balls.

Prepare the beignet mix according to the package directions and heat the oil in a medium saucepot to 350 degrees.

Dip the crawfish balls into the beignet batter and then cook until golden brown, about 6 to 7 minutes. Dust with powdered sugar and serve.

Serves 4

Meander Daze, *by James Michalopoulos,*
courtesy Michalopoulos Gallery.

Delta Feast, *by Sheila Stott Gourlay, courtesy Soren Christensen Gallery.*

BUCKWHEAT CREPES WITH SHRIMP AND LUMP CRABMEAT

Recipe courtesy of Matt Guidry from Meauxbar.

BUCKWHEAT CREPES

- 1/3 cup flour
- 1 1/2 cups buckwheat flour*
- 3 eggs
- 3/4 cup milk
- 1 1/2 cups water
- 1/4 teaspoon salt
- 4 tablespoons canola oil

SHRIMP FILLING

- 2 cups chicken stock
- 2 cups dry white wine
- 1 pound shrimp, peeled, deveined, and cut into 1/2-inch pieces
- 7 1/2 tablespoons butter, divided
- 1 1/2 cups cubed carrots (1/2-inch cubes)
- 1 tablespoon sugar
  Salt and black pepper to taste
- 1/4 cup water
- 10 button mushrooms, rinsed well and thinly sliced
- 4 tablespoons cognac
- 4 tablespoons all-purpose flour
- 1 cup boiling milk
- 1 teaspoon lemon juice
- 1 egg yolk
- 1/2 cup heavy cream

TO ASSEMBLE

- 1 pound jumbo lump crabmeat
- 1/4 cup sliced green onion tops
- 2 tablespoons chopped tarragon
- 1/2 cup grated Gruyére cheese
  Salt and pepper to taste
- 1 egg yolk plus 1 tablespoon water, combined well with a fork
- 6 tablespoons butter, softened for brushing

To make the crepes, combine all ingredients in a bowl and whisk until smooth. Refrigerate batter for at least 1 hour, preferably overnight. Follow instruction to make crepes on page 64.

To make the filling, combine chicken stock and wine in a pot and bring to a boil. Add shrimp to the pot and poach, simmering gently until the shrimp curl and turn pink; drain well, reserving poaching liquid for sauce. Refresh shrimp in an ice bath; drain well.

In a saucepan, combine 1 1/2 tablespoons butter, carrots, sugar, salt, pepper, and water. Bring to a boil over high heat and cook uncovered until water is evaporated and carrots are tender and slightly caramelized.

Recipe continued on page 74

* Buckwheat flour can be purchased online at: www.thebirkettmills.com.

Heat 2 tablespoons butter in a sautée pan over medium-high heat until frothy. Add mushrooms and cook until nicely browned and caramelized. Add cognac and light to flambé. Reduce liqueur completely.

In a saucepan over medium heat, melt remaining butter until frothy. Add flour, whisking to combine well. Cook for 1 minute, stirring to dispel the flour taste. Add boiling milk in a slow stream, whisking to combine. Add 1 cup of the reserved poaching liquid in a slow stream, whisking to combine. Add lemon juice and continue to whisk until all ingredients are well combined and sauce is smooth and thick.

Beat egg yolk and cream in a mixing bowl. Add 1 tablespoon of the sauce to the egg cream mixture, whisking to combine. Continue to add 1 tablespoon of sauce to the egg cream mixture until half of the sauce has been combined. Pour the "tempered" egg mixture into the saucepan with the remaining sauce and return to heat. Stir continually until the temperature reaches 170 degrees. Do not boil!

To assemble, combine in a large mixing bowl, the shrimp, crabmeat, caramelized carrots, sautéed mushrooms, green onions, and tarragon with the sauce; fold the ingredients to combine. Add the cheese, salt, and pepper and continue folding until combined.

Place 4 tablespoons filling in the center of each crepe. Evenly disperse the filling from end to end of crepe approximately 1¹/₂ inches in height and thickness. Roll crepe tightly around the filling. With your finger, spread a little egg wash on the ending edge of the crepe and place on a lightly buttered sheetpan with the seam side down. Brush the crepes lightly with butter and bake in a 475-degree oven for 10 minutes, or until the crepes are crispy and filling is bubbling hot. Serve immediately.

Serves 6

SMOKED SALMON SLAW

Recipe courtesy of Corbin Evans.

- 1 tablespoon brown sugar
- 4 teaspoons kosher salt
- 1/8 teaspoon paprika
- 4 (3-ounce) salmon fillets
- 1/8 teaspoon freshly ground black pepper
- 3 cups shredded green cabbage
- 1 carrot, grated
- 1/2 cup Creole Mustard Vinaigrette (see below)

CREOLE MUSTARD VINAIGRETTE

- 1 tablespoon Creole mustard
- 1 tablespoon Dijon mustard
- 2 tablespoons roasted garlic
- 2 tablespoons rice vinegar
- 1/4 cup canola oil
- 1 tablespoon water
  Salt and pepper to taste

Combine the brown sugar, salt, and paprika and rub evenly over the salmon. Season with black pepper. Allow to sit, refrigerated, for 12 to 18 hours. Rinse the salmon and pat dry. Prepare a stovetop smoker and smoke salmon until cooked to desired internal temperature, about 6 to 8 minutes for medium rare.

Combine cabbage and carrot and dress with the vinaigrette. Flake the smoked salmon over top and serve.

To make the vinaigrette, combine all ingredients except for the oil, water, salt, and pepper. Slowly whisk in the oil in a steady stream. If the vinaigrette is too thick, whisk in the water. Season with salt and pepper.

Serves 4

SMOKED DUCK BREAST PAIN PERDU WITH FONTINA CHEESE AND CANE SYRUP

Recipes courtesy of Greg Picolo The Bistro at the Maison de Ville.

4 to 6 duck breasts
1 tablespoon salt
2 teaspoons pepper
2 teaspoons raw sugar

PAIN PERDU

3 cups half-and-half
3 eggs, slightly beaten
3 tablespoons granulated sugar
1 1/2 teaspoons cinnamon
1/2 teaspoon bourbon vanilla extract
1 teaspoon salt
1/2 teaspoon cayenne pepper
1/2 teaspoon ancho chile powder
1 teaspoon granulated garlic
8 to 12 (1-inch-thick) slices French
     bread (2 pieces per person)
1/4 cup butter

SYRUP

4 tablespoons butter
1 cup orange juice
1 1/2 cups Steen's pure cane syrup
     Tabasco sauce to taste

8 to 12 (1/2-inch-thick) slices Fontina
     or Havarti cheese

Season the duck breast with salt, pepper, and sugar. Let rest overnight in the refrigerator, then cold smoke, for 15 to 20 minutes. The smoking process is for flavoring. Roast meat at 475 degrees for 12 minutes until medium-rare, rest 3 to 4 minutes prior to slicing.

To make the pain perdu, combine all ingredients except bread and butter. Place bread slices in mixture and allow to absorb liquid. Do not allow bread to get soggy or it will fall apart when sautéing. Sautée bread in butter until golden brown, springy to the touch, and cooked in middle.

To make the syrup, combine all ingredients in a saucepan and simmer 1 to 2 minutes to reduce slightly.

To assemble, slice the duck and arrange on top of the pain perdu, top with cheese slices and broil until melted. Top with syrup and serve.

Serves 4 to 6

Note: Sunny side up eggs would be a great complement and will also enhance the brunch aspect of the dish.

Tractor, *by Jim Sudduth, courtesy Anton Haardt Gallery.*

Redish Egret, *by Leslie Staub, courtesy LeMieux Galleries.*

HICKORY-SMOKED SOFT-SHELL CRAB WITH NEW POTATO SALAD

Recipe courtesy of Corbin Evans.

4   soft-shell crabs, cleaned and rinsed
1   cup all-purpose flour
2/3 cup corn flour
1/3 cup cornmeal
1   tablespoon Savvy Spice or
     Creole seasoning
     Canola or peanut oil
2   cups buttermilk

NEW POTATO SALAD

1   pound red-skinned new potatoes
1/4 cup red wine vinegar
2   bay leaves
     Kosher salt
1   hard-boiled egg, peeled and diced
2   green onions, diced
1/4 cup Blue Plate or other mayonnaise
1/4 cup sour cream
2   to 3 stalks celery, chopped
1   tablespoon Creole mustard
1/4 cup finely chopped dill pickle
2   tablespoons chopped flat-leaf parsley

Smoke soft-shell crabs according to stovetop smoker directions using hickory chips for 8 to 10 minutes, depending on the size of the crabs.

Combine the flour, corn flour, and corn meal with the seasoning and mix to blend well. Heat a large heavy-bottomed skillet over medium-high heat and add oil to coat the pan. Dip the crabs in the buttermilk and then dredge in the breading mixture. Carefully place crabs in the pan and cook until golden, about 2 to 3 minutes. Turn over and cook 2 to 3 minutes more, or until cooked through and golden brown.

To make the potato salad, place potatoes in a large saucepan and cover with cold water. Add vinegar, bay leaves, and salt. Bring to a gentle boil; simmer for 15 to 20 minutes, or until just tender. Drain well and then quarter or halve the potatoes.

In a large mixing bowl, combine the remaining ingredients. Add the potatoes and toss to coat. Serve immediately or refrigerate . Set the crab on top of the salad and serve.

Serves 4

EGGS FLORENTINE

Recipe courtesy of Mary Ann Meyer.

1	pound fresh spinach
	Water
1 1/2	cups heavy cream, divided
	Salt and pepper to taste
1	package frozen artichoke hearts, defrosted and chopped
2	tablespoons butter
6	eggs

Egret, by Leslie Staub, courtesy LeMieux Galleries.

Facing page: Little Blue Heron, *by Leslie Staub, courtesy LeMieux Galleries.*

Preheat oven to 350 degrees.

Cook spinach in a little water for 2 minutes, and then drain and chop. In a medium sautée pan, add cooked spinach and cook about 3 to 5 minutes more. Add 3/4 cup heavy cream, and then season with salt and pepper. Add artichoke hearts and cook another 2 to 3 minutes.

Using the butter, grease a 9 x 13-inch casserole dish. Pour the spinach artichoke mixture into the pan and then make 6 pockets for the eggs. Crack 1 egg into each pocket and then spoon 1 to 2 tablespoons heavy cream over each egg. Bake for 8 minutes, or until eggs have set. Serve with toasted bread.

Serves 6

Salads

B.L.T. Salad

Recipe courtesy of Greg Picolo from The Bistro at The Maison de Ville.

1 pound apple-smoked bacon, cut
   into lardoons, or thinly sliced
1 tablespoon Dijon mustard
2 teaspoons minced garlic
1 teaspoon chopped rosemary
1/2 teaspoon chopped tarragon
1 1/2 teaspoons Worcestershire sauce
1 teaspoon soy sauce
1 teaspoon horseradish
1 cup olive oil
2 tablespoons mayonnaise
24 ounces mixed greens
4 to 6 hard-boiled eggs, sliced into quarters
3 Creole or other tomatoes, sliced

In a medium sautée pan over medium heat, cook bacon until almost crispy. Reserve 1/4 cup of the bacon drippings. Drain bacon on paper towels.

Combine the Dijon mustard, garlic, rosemary, tarragon, Worcestershire sauce, soy sauce, horseradish, and olive oil. Fold in mayonnaise.

In a medium mixing bowl, toss the mixed greens with the dressing. Divide the greens equally between individual serving plates and alternate tomato slices and egg quarters around the plate. Sprinkle with the reserved bacon. Drizzle a little of the warm bacon fat over top.

Serves 4 to 6

If We Lived By The River, by James Michalopoulos, courtesy Michalopoulos Gallery.

Pelican Landing on Water, *by Archie Bonge, courtesy Bonge Foundation and the Ogden Museum of Southern Art.*

LOUISIANA CREOLE TOMATO SALAD WITH SAUTÉED SHRIMP AND PEPPER JELLY VINAIGRETTE

Recipe courtesy of Chuck Subra from La Côte Brasserie.

1 1/2 tablespoons minced garlic, divided
1 1/2 tablespoons minced shallots, divided
   4 tablespoons pepper jelly
   2 ounces champagne vinegar
   1 tablespoon chopped basil
 1/4 cup olive oil
 1/2 cup vegetable oil
     Salt and pepper to taste
   6 tablespoons butter
   2 pounds Louisiana shrimp, peeled
     and deveined
   6 Creole tomatoes, sliced and drained
     on paper towels
   1 tablespoon chopped chives

In a small mixing bowl, combine 1 tablespoon garlic, 1 tablespoon shallots, pepper jelly, vinegar, and basil. Mix thoroughly then add oils. Season with salt and pepper.

In a medium saucepan over medium high heat, melt butter and add the shrimp and remaining garlic and shallots. Cook the shrimp for 3 to 4 minutes, or until cooked through. Season with salt and pepper.

To serve, place tomato slices on the bottom of each plate. Season the slices with salt and pepper. Place the sautéed shrimp in the center of the tomato slices and spoon the dressing over the shrimp and tomatoes. Garnish with the chopped chives. Serve immediately.

Serves 6 to 8

ROASTED BEET SALAD WITH BELGIAN ENDIVE, TWO DRESSINGS, GOAT CHEESE, AND WALNUTS

Recipe courtesy of Stephen G. Schwarz from Mat and Naddie's Restaurant.

2 pounds red beets, greens removed
2 tablespoons olive oil
Salt and pepper to taste
1/4 cup water
1 teaspoon fennel seeds
1 teaspoon coriander seeds
1/2 teaspoon sugar
1/2 teaspoon salt
1/4 teaspoon freshly ground black pepper
1/4 cup rice wine vinegar
1/2 cup walnut oil
1/4 pound goat cheese
2 ounces walnuts, crushed
2 heads Belgian endive, julienned
1 red onion, finely diced to garnish
1 fennel bulb top, finely diced to garnish
1 cup Creole Mustard-Cane Syrup Vinaigrette (see below)

CREOLE MUSTARD–CANE SYRUP VINAIGRETTE

1/4 cup Creole mustard
1/3 cup cider vinegar
2 tablespoons cane syrup
2 teaspoons chopped fresh rosemary
2 teaspoons chopped fresh thyme
2/3 teaspoon cayenne pepper
2 teaspoons salt
2/3 teaspoon minced garlic
1 cup canola oil
2/3 cup sliced shallots (sliced into rings)

Preheat oven to 350 degrees. Line a shallow baking dish with aluminum foil. Toss beets with the olive oil and season with salt and pepper. Add water to the pan and cover with foil. Roast at 350 degrees for 30 to 40 minutes, or until tender. Remove the beets and allow to cool. When cool enough to handle, use a paper towel to remove the skins—it should come off easily. Slice the beets into 1/8-inch-thick half moons.

In a sautée pan, toast the fennel and coriander seeds until they begin to pop. Finely grind in a spice grinder or use a mortar and pestle. Toss the beets with the spices, sugar, salt, and pepper.

In a mixing bowl, whisk together vinegar and walnut oil. Pour over beets and toss to coat. Add goat cheese, walnuts, and endive; mix gently. Divide salad among four plates and drizzle with the vinaigrette. Garnish with red onion and fennel. Serve immediately.

To make the vinaigrette, whisk all ingredients together except oil and shallots. When well combined, slowly whisk in the oil and the shallots.

Serves 4

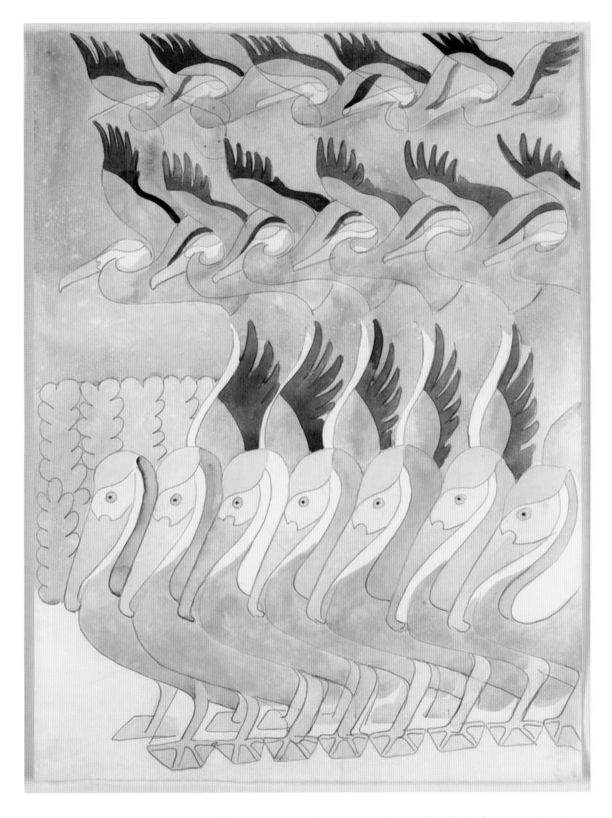

Pelicans, by Walter Andersen, *courtesy Andersen Family and the Ogden Museum of Southern Art.*

Fable #1, *by Nicole Charbonnet, courtesy Arthur Roger Gallery.*

PRYTANIA SALAD

Recipe courtesy of Rich and Danielle Sutton from The St. James Cheese Company.

1   pound baby lettuce
    White Balsamic Vinaigrette (see below)
    Salt and freshly ground black pepper
      to taste
4   red or gold beets, cooked, skinned,
     and sliced
2   Bittersweet Plantation Evangeline Goat's
     Cheese or 8 ounces local goat cheese
1 1/2 cups Louisiana or other pecan halves
1   cup golden raisins

WHITE BALSAMIC VINAIGRETTE

1   tablespoon Dijon mustard
1   tablespoon white balsamic vinegar
1   teaspoon water
1/2 cup olive oil
    Salt and pepper to taste

Wash and dry the lettuce. In a large salad bowl, toss the lettuce with the White Balsamic Vinaigrette, coating all the leaves; season with a little salt and pepper. Equally divide the greens among four plates. Arrange equal portions of the beets along the edges of the salad; crumble the goat cheese over top of each salad followed by the pecans and raisins. Serve with slices of crusty French bread.

To make the vinaigrette, stir together the mustard, vinegar, and water in a small mixing bowl. Slowly whisk in the olive oil in a steady stream. Continue whisking until mixture is thick and creamy. Season with salt and pepper.

Serves 4

BRUSSELS SPROUT SALAD

Recipe courtesy of Ryan Hughes from Café Degas.

2 pounds Brussels sprouts
4 slices thick-cut bacon, cut into small pieces
1/4 cup sherry vinegar
1/2 cup corn syrup
1 cup olive oil
   Salt and pepper to taste
1 red onion, thinly sliced
1/4 pound Stilton cheese
2 teaspoons chopped fresh mint
2 teaspoons chopped tarragon

Remove the tough outer layers from the Brussels sprouts and slice in half. In a large pot of boiling salted water, add the Brussels sprouts. Cook for 2 to 3 minutes, or until just tender; immediately submerge into a bowl of ice water. Once cool, remove the Brussels sprouts and place on a sheetpan lined with paper towels.

In a medium sautée pan over low heat, render the bacon until crisp. Remove the bacon and set aside. Add the Brussels sprouts to the pan and cook until light brown.

In a small mixing bowl, mix the vinegar with the corn syrup. Slowly add the olive oil in a steady stream. Season with salt and pepper.

Toss the Brussels sprouts with the red onion and bacon. Add the vinaigrette and gently toss in the Stilton cheese. Sprinkle with the chopped herbs. Serve warm.

Serves 4

Clementine Picking Cotton, *by Clementine Hunter, courtesy the Whitecloud Foundation and the Ogden Museum of Southern Art.*

Untitled painting, *by Will Henry Stevens, courtesy Blue Spiral Gallery and the Ogden Museum of Southern Art.*

PROSCIUTTO AND MELON SALAD WITH RICOTTA SALATA

Recipe courtesy of Stacey Meyer.

1 ripe cantaloupe, honeydew, or Galia
  melon
2 tablespoons champagne vinegar
1 teaspoon chopped mint
1/2 cup olive oil
  Sea salt and freshly ground black
  pepper to taste
2 bunches mizuna lettuce or watercress
1/2 pound San Danielle prosciutto,
  thinly sliced
1 cup crumbled ricotta salata

Cut the melon into quarters, and then remove the seeds and the rind. Using a mandolin or a sharp knife, slice the melon into thin ribbons.

In a small mixing bowl, combine the vinegar, mint and olive oil. Whisk to combine and season with salt and pepper. Toss the greens with half of the vinaigrette.

To serve, divide greens equally between four plates. Top with equal portions of the melon, prosciutto and ricotta salata. Drizzle the remaining vinaigrette on each salad and serve.

Serves 4

GRILLED SCALLOP AND JUMBO LUMP CRAB "SANDWICH" WITH FRISEE, AVOCADO AND CITRUS THYME VINAIGRETTE

Recipe courtesy of Chef Greg Picolo from The Bistro at The Maison de Ville.

1/2 cup rice vinegar
1 tablespoon chopped thyme
1 lime, juiced
1 lemon, juiced
3 teaspoons Creole or grainy mustard
1 teaspoon Worcestershire sauce
1 1/4 cups olive oil
    Salt and pepper to taste
1/2 pound jumbo lump crabmeat
4 to 6 large scallops (10-count, preferably),
    sliced in half
1 head frisee
1 large Haas avocado, thinly sliced
    White truffle oil (optional)

Combine the vinegar, thyme, juices, mustard, and Worcestershire sauce; mix well. Slowly whisk in the olive oil and season with salt and pepper.

Lightly toss crab with some salt and pepper and 4 tablespoons of the vinaigrette.

Grill scallops 1 minute on each side.

Arrange frisee and avocado artfully on plate. Place 1 slice of scallop on each plate and top with 1/4 cup crab mixture then top with a second scallop slice to form a "sandwich." Drizzle truffle oil lightly around plate and spoon some of the vinaigrette over the scallops and serve.

Serves 4 to 6

Garden Spirit,
by Lisa "Tinka" Jordy, courtesy
Carol Robinson Gallery.

French Quarter Rooftops From This Studio, *by Sven August Knute Heldner, courtesy Paulette Holahan and Franz Heldner and the Ogden Museum of Southern Art.*

ASPARAGUS SALAD WITH SERRANO HAM, MARINATED CHERRY TOMATOES AND MANCHEGO CHEESE

Recipe courtesy of Rich and Danielle Sutton from St. James Cheese Company.

1   large bunch thick asparagus (25 to 30 spears)
2   cups red and yellow cherry tomatoes, halved and quartered
2   tablespoons red wine vinegar
1   tablespoon extra virgin olive oil
    Basil, chiffonade
    Salt and freshly ground black pepper to taste
    Dijon Vinaigrette (see below)
3/4 cup grated manchego cheese
1/2 pound serrano ham, very thinly sliced and julienned

DIJON VINAIGRETTE

1   tablespoon Dijon mustard
1   tablespoon red wine vinegar
1   teaspoon water
1/4 cup to 1/2 cup olive oil
    Salt and pepper to taste

Trim asparagus spears of tough ends. Bring a large pot of salted water to a boil and then remove from heat. Put asparagus spears in the just boiled water to sit for 15 minutes. Remove asparagus and place in a salted ice water bath. Asparagus can be made ahead of time and refrigerated.

Place tomatoes in a small bowl. Toss with vinegar, olive oil, basil, salt, and pepper, set aside.

Divide the asparagus evenly between four plates. Drizzle the vinaigrette over asparagus. Evenly distribute the cherry tomato mixture over the plates. Sprinkle the manchego cheese over the tomatoes. Top the dish with the ham and black pepper.

To make the vinaigrette, mix the mustard, vinegar, and water together in a mixing bowl. Slowly add the olive oil in a steady stream while whisking. Blend until pale and creamy. Season with salt and pepper.

Serves 4

SPINACH SALAD WITH AVOCADO AND PINK GRAPEFRUIT

Recipe courtesy of Stacey Meyer.

1/2 cup walnut pieces
2 tablespoons walnut oil
1 teaspoon minced shallot
2 tablespoons white balsamic vinegar
1/2 cup extra virgin olive oil
Sea salt and freshly ground black pepper
to taste
1 1/2 pounds baby spinach
1 pink grapefruit, sectioned
1 avocado, peeled and thinly sliced

In a small sautée pan, toast the walnut pieces in the walnut oil.

In a large mixing bowl, whisk the shallot, vinegar, and oil. Season with salt and pepper. Add the spinach, grapefruit, and avocado; toss to coat.

Divide the salad evenly among four plates. Top with the walnuts and walnut oil. Top with freshly ground black pepper if desired.

Serves 4

Knoll, *by Michael Marlowe, courtesy Soren Christensen Gallery.*

HARICOTS VERTS WITH TONNATO SAUCE

Recipe courtesy of Stacey Meyer.

1 1/2   pounds haricots verts
2   ripe Heirloom tomatoes, sliced
Tonnato Sauce (see below)
Fleur de sel or kosher salt and freshly
cracked black pepper to taste

TONNATO SAUCE

1/2   pound fresh tuna, cooked through
4   anchovies
1/8   cup capers
2   tablespoons lemon juice
1   cup extra virgin olive oil
1 1/2   cups mayonnaise

In a large pot of salted boiling water, cook the haricots verts 3 to 4 minutes, or until tender. Remove the haricots verts from the boiling water and place directly into a bowl of salted ice water. When cool, place on a sheetpan lined with paper towels to drain. Haricots verts may be cooked ahead and refrigerated.

Divide the slices of tomato among four plates; place the haricots verts on top of the tomatoes and spoon the Tonnato Sauce over top. Season with Fleur de sel and pepper.

To make the Tonnato Sauce, combine all ingredients except the mayonnaise in a food processor until smooth. Fold the mixture into the mayonnaise. If necessary, adjust the seasoning by adding more lemon juice, salt, and pepper. Extra sauce can be stored in the refrigerator for several days.

Serves 4

Madisonville, *by Jason Langley,*
courtesy Jason Langley.

SHRIMP REMOULADE

Recipe courtesy of Brian Landry, Executive Chef Galatoire's Restaurant, from Galatoire's: Biography of a Bistro, by Marda Burton and Kenneth Holditch (Hill Street Press).

3/4 cup chopped celery

3/4 cup chopped scallions, white and green parts

1/2 cup chopped curly parsley

1 cup chopped yellow onion

1/2 cup ketchup

1/2 cup tomato purée

1/2 cup Creole mustard or any coarse, grainy brown mustard

2 tablespoons prepared horseradish to taste

1/4 cup red wine vinegar

2 tablespoons Spanish hot paprika

1 teaspoon Worcestershire sauce

1/2 cup salad oil

4 dozen jumbo (15-count) shrimp, peeled, boiled and chilled

1 small head iceberg lettuce, washed, dried, and cut into thin ribbons

Mince the celery, scallions, parsley, and onion in a food processor. Add the ketchup, tomato purée, Creole mustard, horseradish, vinegar, paprika, and Worcestershire sauce. Begin processing again and add the oil in a slow drizzle to emulsify. Stop when the dressing is smooth. Chill for 6 to 8 hours or overnight. Correct the seasoning with additional horseradish, if desired, after the ingredients have had the opportunity to marry.

In a large mixing bowl, add the sauce to the shrimp and toss gently to coat. Divide the lettuce among six chilled salad plates. Divide the shrimp evenly over the lettuce and serve.

Serves 6

Solara and White Rocking Chairs, Laurel Street, *by Phil Sandusky, courtesy Cole Pratt Gallery.*

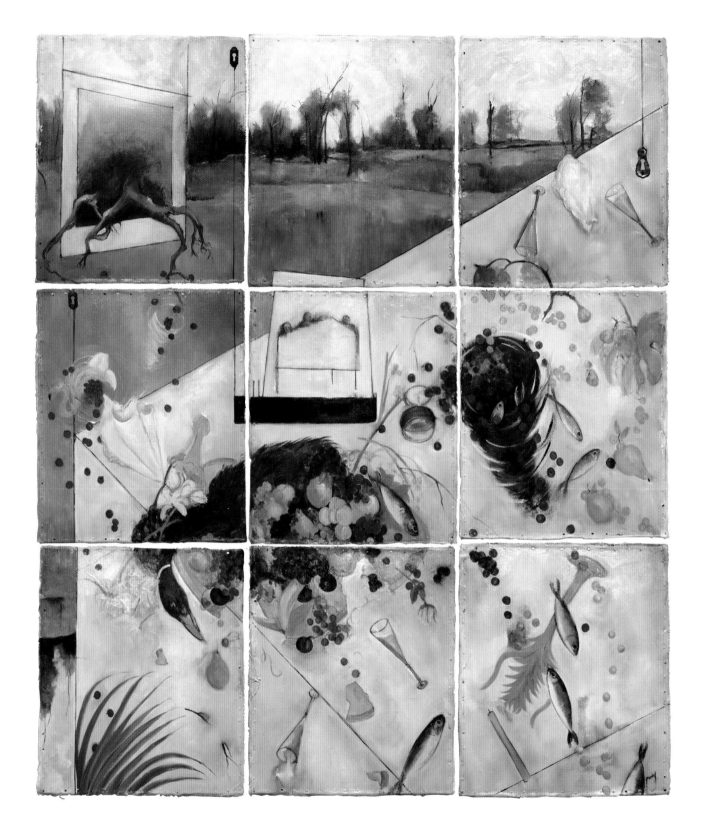

Disconnect, *by Sheila Stott Gourlay, courtesy Soren Christensen Gallery.*

CORN MACQUE CHOUX

Recipe courtesy of John Folse from The Encyclopedia of Cajun & Creole Cuisine
(Chef John Folse & Company Publishing).

8 ears fresh corn
1/2 cup bacon drippings
1 cup diced onions
1/2 cup diced celery
1/2 cup diced green bell peppers
1/2 cup diced red bell peppers
1/4 cup minced garlic
1/4 cup minced andouille sausage
2 cups chopped tomatoes
2 tablespoons tomato sauce
2 cups (150- to 200-count) shrimp, peeled
   and deveined
1 cup sliced green onions
   Salt and freshly ground black pepper
   to taste

Select tender, well-developed ears of corn and shuck. Using a sharp knife, cut kernels from the cob. Scrape each cob again to remove all "milk" (juice remaining on cob) and additional pulp from corn. The richness of this dish will depend on how much milk and pulp can be scraped from the cobs.

In a 3-quart cast-iron Dutch oven, melt bacon drippings over medium-high heat. Sautée corn, onions, celery, bell peppers, garlic, and andouille sausage for 15 to 20 minutes, or until vegetables are wilted and corn is tender. Stir in tomatoes, tomato sauce, and shrimp. Cook for another 15 to 20 minutes, or until juice from tomatoes and shrimp is rendered into the dish. Add green onions and then season with salt and pepper. Continue to cook 15 minutes more and then serve.

Serves 8

WILD RICE SALAD

Recipe courtesy of Mary Ann Meyer.

2 (4-ounce) boxes wild rice
8 to 10 sun-dried tomatoes, sliced
1/2 cup cured black olives, pitted
1/2 cup toasted pecan halves
1/2 cup extra virgin olive oil
1/4 cup balsamic vinegar
2 tablespoons chopped oregano
Baby spinach (optional)

Cook wild rice according to directions on package; drain and cool on a sheetpan. Combine rice, tomatoes, olives, pecans, oil, vinegar, and oregano. Toss to coat. Serve alone or over baby spinach.

Serves 4 to 6

Mrs. Henry's Funeral Can't See Her Face for the Flowers, *by Clementine Hunter, courtesy the Whitecloud Foundation and the Ogden Museum of Southern Art.*

Uptown Street, *by Lulu King Saxon, courtesy Ogden Museum of Southern Art.*

Soups

GAZPACHO

Recipe courtesy of Ken Smith.

4 large tomatoes, cored and chopped
1 red bell pepper, stemmed, seeded, and chopped
1 green bell pepper, stemmed, seeded, and chopped
1 small red onion, chopped
3 cups tomato juice, divided
1 cup cubed good-quality bread
1/2 cucumber, chopped
1 lime, juiced
1 tablespoon Worcestershire sauce
1/2 teaspoon Tabasco sauce
1 head garlic, roasted
1/2 cup olive oil
1/4 cup red wine vinegar
   Salt and freshly ground black pepper to taste

Place tomatoes, bell peppers, and onion in a blender with 1 cup tomato juice and blend. Add the bread. When smooth, pour mixture into a large bowl.

Blend the remaining ingredients until smooth and add to the bowl. Adjust the Tabasco and Worcestershire sauces if necessary. Refrigerate until cold and then serve.

Serves 4

Brennan's at Night, *by Alan Flattman, courtesy Bryant Galleries.*

Untitled painting, *by Dusti Bonge, courtesy Bonge Foundation.*

OYSTER STEW WITH CARAMELIZED ONIONS AND PARMESAN TOASTS

Recipe courtesy of Matt Guidry from Meauxbar.

3 tablespoons olive oil
1 1/2 tablespoons unsalted butter
2 Spanish or yellow onions, thinly sliced
1 1/2 tablespoons sugar
4 cloves garlic, finely diced
4 cups oyster juice or clam juice
3 Yukon gold potatoes, skin on and cut into 1/2-inch dice
1 1/2 cups heavy cream
1/3 cup Crème Fraîche (see below)
Salt and freshly ground black pepper to taste
66 oysters, shucked
2 tablespoons finely chopped fresh tarragon

CRÈME FRAÎCHE
1 cup heavy cream
1 tablespoon buttermilk

PARMESAN TOASTS
1 clove garlic
Olive oil
6 pistolettes, quartered long way, end to end
Grated Parmesan cheese

Heat olive oil and butter in a saucepan over medium heat. Add the onions and sugar and cook until the onions are caramelized. Add the garlic and cook for 2 minutes. Add the oyster juice to the onions and bring to a boil. Add potatoes and cook 5 minutes. Add heavy cream and bring to a simmer. Whisk in crème fraîche. Season with salt and pepper. Add oysters and tarragon and cook just until oyster edges curl.

For the crème fraîche, heat heavy cream to 95 degrees and combine with buttermilk in a container with lid cocked. Let sit at room temperature for 24 hours before refrigerating.

For the Parmesan Toasts, preheat oven to 400 degrees.

Smash garlic with the side of a knife and mince well. Combine with olive oil in a small mixing bowl. Brush garlic oil onto pistolette quarters and sprinkle generously with Parmesan cheese. Toast in the oven for 2 to 3 minutes, or until toasts are golden.

Serves 6

CHICKEN AND SAUSAGE GUMBO

Recipe courtesy of John Folse from The Encyclopedia of Cajun & Creole Cuisine
(Chef John Folse & Company Publishing).

1   (5-pound) stewing hen
1   pound smoked sausage or
        andouille sausage
1   cup oil
1 1/2   cups flour
2   cups diced onions
2   cups diced celery
1   cup diced green bell peppers
1/4   cup minced garlic
3   quarts chicken stock
24   button mushrooms
2   cups sliced green onions
1   bay leaf
        Sprig of thyme
1   tablespoon chopped basil
        Salt and freshly cracked black
            pepper to taste
        Louisiana hot sauce to taste
1/2   cup chopped parsley
        Cooked white rice

Using a sharp boning knife, cut the hen into 8 to 10 serving pieces. Remove as much fat as possible. Cut sausage into 1/2-inch slices and set aside.

In a 2-gallon stockpot, heat oil over medium-high heat. Whisk in flour, stirring constantly until a golden brown roux is achieved. Stir in onions, celery, bell peppers, and garlic. Sautée 3 to 5 minutes, or until vegetables are wilted. Blend chicken and sausage into vegetable mixture, and sautée approximately 15 minutes. Add chicken stock, one ladle at a time, stirring constantly. Bring to a rolling boil, reduce to a simmer and cook approximately 1 hour. Skim any fat or oil that rises to the top. Stir in mushrooms, green onions, bay leaf, thyme, and basil. Season to taste using salt, pepper, and hot sauce. Cook an additional 1 to 2 hours, if necessary, or until chicken is tender and falling apart. Stir in parsley and adjust seasonings. Serve over hot white rice.

Note: You may wish to boil chicken 1 to 2 hours before beginning gumbo. Reserve stock, bone chicken and use meat and stock in gumbo.

Serves 8 to 10

Chef and Rooster, by Campbell Hutchinson, courtesy Soren Christensen Gallery.

Stork Plate Design, *by Dusti Bonge, courtesy Bonge Foundation.*

OYSTER AND ARTICHOKE SOUP

Recipe courtesy of Mary Ann Meyer.

1   stick butter
1   bunch green onions, minced
2   cloves garlic, minced
2   (14-ounce) cans artichoke hearts or
      bottoms, drained and chopped
3   tablespoons flour
4   cups chicken stock
      Worcestershire sauce
      Pinch of dried thyme
1   quart oysters, chopped

In a large saucepan, melt butter; sautée green onions and garlic for 3 to 4 minutes and then add the artichoke. Cook for another 3 minutes. Add flour and cook for 2 to 3 minutes. Add chicken stock, Worcestershire sauce, and dried thyme. Simmer for 20 minutes. Add the oysters along with their liquid and simmer for 15 to 20 minutes more, or just until the oysters begin to curl slightly around the edges. Do not let the soup boil. Serve immediately with crusty French bread.

Serves 4

PARISIAN ONION SOUP

Recipe courtesy of Matt Guidry from Meauxbar.

4 medium onions, thinly sliced
4 tablespoons butter
4 tablespoons flour
1/2 cup white wine
1 quart beef stock
  French bread, sliced thin and cut to
    fit the diameter of the soup crocks
  Grated Parmesan cheese
  Parsley, chopped

In a saucepan, sautée the onions in butter over medium-high heat until well browned, about 30 minutes. Sprinkle with flour and stir well to combine. Cook over low heat for 10 minutes to dispel the flour taste. Deglaze with white wine and bring to a quick boil; reduce until almost dry. Add the beef stock to the onions and bring to a boil. Simmer until the onions are tender, about 15 minutes. Ladle 1 cup of onion soup into a soup crock. Float a slice of toast on the soup. Mound and then level 3 heaping tablespoons of grated cheese on top. Place the crock under a broiler until the cheese melts and browns. Garnish with parsley. Serve immediately.

Serves 4

DANDELION BISQUE

Recipe courtesy of Stephen G. Schwarz from Mat and Naddies.

1 bunch dandelion greens, chicory,
   or curly endive
1/4 cup butter, divided
1/2 cup chicken stock
1/2 large Spanish or yellow onion
1/2 small carrot, chopped
2 tablespoons flour
2 cups milk
2/3 teaspoon freshly ground black pepper
   or to taste
1/2 cup heavy cream
1 1/2 teaspoons Dijon mustard
1/2 cup croutons
1/4 to 1/3 cup bacon bits

In a large pot of salted boiling water, blanch the dandelion greens for 1 to 2 minutes. Immediately remove from the boiling water to a bowl of ice water. When cool, gently squeeze the greens of excess water and chop.

In a large saucepan, melt half the butter over medium heat. When bubbling, add the greens and cook for 15 minutes, or until all the moisture has evaporated. Add the chicken stock and reduce by half.

In another large saucepan, melt the remaining butter. Add onion and carrot and sweat until very soft. Add the flour and cook 2 to 3 minutes. Whisk in the milk and cook for 20 to 25 minutes, stirring continually. Add the greens with the reduced stock to the milk and remove from heat. When cool, purée in a blender.

Combine cream and mustard; whisk into soup. Serve the soup hot with the croutons and bacon bits sprinkled over top.

Serves 4 to 6

CARROT VICHYSSOISE

Recipe courtesy of Ryan Hughes from Café Degas.

2 tablespoons extra virgin olive oil
1 leek, washed and sliced into rounds
1/2 Spanish or yellow onion, sliced
1 stalk celery, chopped
1 teaspoon chopped garlic
4 carrots, peeled and chopped
1 russet potato, peeled and diced
1 quart chicken stock
1 bay leaf
Salt and pepper to taste
2 tablespoons Orange Blossom water*
1/4 cup heavy cream
2 tablespoons thinly sliced chives or
whole chive blossoms

In a large saucepan over medium heat, add the olive oil. When hot, add the leek, onion, celery, and garlic; cook for 5 minutes, or until the vegetables are very tender. Add the carrots, potato, chicken stock, and bay leaf; cook for 35 to 40 minutes. Remove from heat and cool slightly. Purée in a blender and strain through a fine mesh sieve and return to pan. Season with salt and pepper. Add the Orange Blossom water and heavy cream and simmer for 10 minutes more. Chill the soup and serve cold garnished with the chives.

Serves 6

* Can be found in the baking aisle at gourmet markets, Middle Eastern markets, or online.

Untitled Kitchens and Dining Rooms, *by Robert Brantley, courtesy Robert Brantley.*

CREOLE TOMATO GAZPACHO

Recipe courtesy of Scott Snodgrass from One.

6 Creole or other tomatoes, chopped
2 yellow squash, seeded and finely diced
2 zucchini, seeded and finely diced
1 red onion, chopped
2 stalks celery, chopped
1 medium carrot, chopped
1 tablespoon chopped garlic
1/8 cup canola oil
1/2 cup red wine vinegar
2 lemons, juiced
2 limes, juiced
1/4 cup julienned basil
Kosher salt and freshly ground black
pepper to taste

In a food processor, purée the tomatoes and pour into a large mixing bowl. Purée half the squash and half the zucchini with the onion, celery, carrot, and garlic. Pour into a mixing bowl. Whisk in the canola oil, vinegar, juices, and basil. Season with salt and pepper. Refrigerate and serve well chilled.

Serves 4

Two Men on a Stoop, *by Shirley Rabe Masinter, courtesy LeMieux Galleries.*

At the Corner, *by Shirley Rabe Masinter, courtesy LeMieux Galleries.*

CORN AND CRAB SOUP

Recipe courtesy of Mary Ann Meyer.

1/4 cup butter
1/4 cup chopped white onion
1/4 cup chopped green onions
2 tablespoons flour
2 cups fresh corn kernels, with their milk
4 cups milk
1 cup heavy cream
Salt and pepper to taste
1 pound lump crabmeat, cleaned

In a large saucepan, melt butter and add onions. Cook for 4 to 5 minutes or until translucent. Add flour and cook for another 2 to 3 minutes. In a blender, purée the corn and its milk; add to the onions and cook for 5 minutes. Add the milk and cream; season with salt and pepper. Bring to a simmer then add crabmeat and allow to heat through. Serve immediately with French bread.

Serves 4

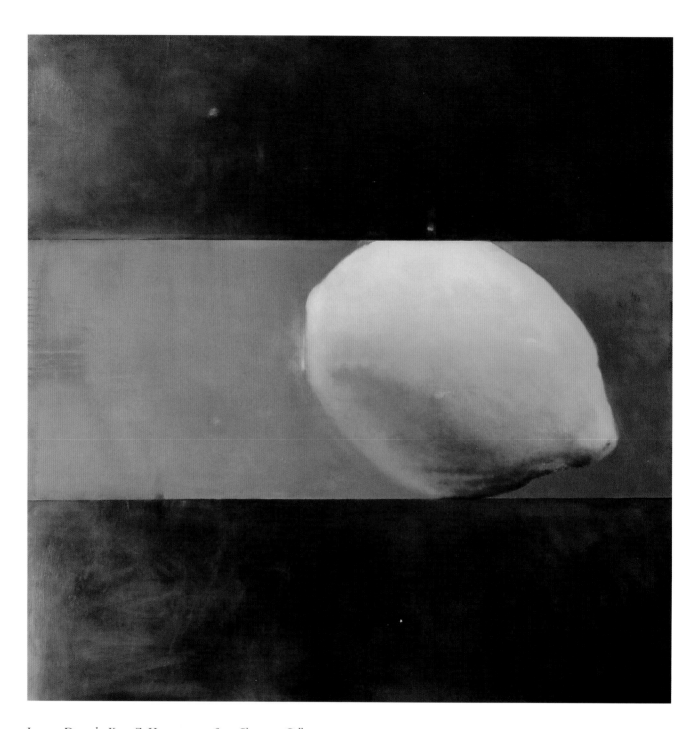

Lemon Drop, *by Karen Z. Haynes, courtesy Soren Christensen Gallery.*

SWEET PEA SOUP

Recipe courtesy of Stacey Meyer.

1 1/2 pounds fresh peas or 2 (10-ounce)
        packages frozen peas
  2 tablespoons butter
  1 white onion, diced
  2 shallots, diced
  1 clove garlic, sliced
  1 quart chicken stock
  2 sprigs lemon thyme
  2 sprigs tarragon
  1 fresh bay leaf
     Salt and freshly ground white
        pepper to taste
1/2 cup fresh spinach leaves
1/4 cup crème fraiche (see page 115)
1/8 cup mint, chiffonade

In a large pot of salted boiling water, cook fresh peas for 2 minutes and immediately remove to a bowl of salted ice water. If using frozen peas, skip this step.

In a large saucepan over medium heat, melt the butter. Add the onion, shallots, and garlic; cook until tender, about 4 minutes. Add chicken stock. Tie the herbs in a bundle with kitchen twine and add to the pot; simmer for 20 minutes. Add peas and simmer for 3 to 5 minutes more. Season with salt and pepper. Remove from heat and remove herb bundle. In a blender, purée vegetables in batches, adding equal parts spinach to each batch. Strain through a fine sieve and then refrigerate. Serve chilled with a dollop of crème fraiche and mint.

Serves 4

VEGETABLE CHEDDAR SOUP

Recipe courtesy of Stacey Meyer.

2 tablespoons butter
1 cup diced Spanish or yellow onions
2 1/2 cups sliced carrots (sliced into rounds)
1 cup diced Yukon gold potatoes
1 cup quartered and sliced zucchini
1/2 cup quartered and sliced yellow squash
2 cups chicken stock
3/4 teaspoon salt
1/4 teaspoon pepper
2 tablespoons flour mixed with 2 tablespoons softened butter
3 cups milk
1 cup grated cheddar cheese, divided
4 thick slices sourdough bread, toasted

In a large saucepan, melt butter, add onions and cook for 2 to 3 minutes. Add the remaining vegetables and cook until tender. Add the chicken stock, salt, and pepper and bring to a boil. Cook for 20 minutes, uncovered. If necessary, add a little more stock. In a blender, purée the mixture then return to the pot. Add flour mixture and milk, stirring until smooth. Cook for another 10 minutes, or until soup is thick. Stir in 3/4 cup cheese.

To serve, ladle equal portions of soup into bowls, top with toasted bread and sprinkle with remaining cheese.

Serves 4

Flooded Field, by Elemore Morgan, courtesy Arthur Roger Gallery.

ASTURIAN WHITE BEAN SOUP

Recipe courtesy of Adolfo Garcia from RioMar and La Boca.

4 tablespoons sliced garlic
1 medium onion, diced
1/2 cup olive oil
1 pound large or giant lima beans
1 smoked ham hock
1 ham end from serrano or prosciutto
1 cup sliced Spanish chorizo or good-
   quality andouille sausage

In a medium saucepan, cook garlic and onion in olive oil until translucent, about 3 minutes. Add remaining ingredients and 6 cups water or enough to cover. Bring to a boil and then turn heat down to simmer; skim and let cook slowly for 2 to 2^1/$_2$ hours. Check seasoning and remove ham hock and ham end before serving.

Serves 4

Small World #20, *by Allison Stewart,*
courtesy Arthur Roger Gallery.

LOBSTER BISQUE

Recipe courtesy of Mary Ann Meyer.

2 (1 1/2-pound) lobsters
1/4 cup butter, divided
1/4 cup brandy
1 cup dry white wine
   Salt and pepper to taste
1 large Spanish or yellow onion, diced
1 bay leaf
1/8 teaspoon thyme
2 cloves garlic, chopped
2 tablespoons flour
4 tablespoons chopped parsley
4 tablespoons minced green onions
1 cup heavy cream

In a large pot of salted boiling water, cook the lobsters for 7 to 10 minutes; reserve water. Remove meat from lobsters and then cut into small pieces; set aside. Using a mallet, break lobster shells into small pieces; place shells into a pot with 1 tablespoon butter. Stir shells over high heat, add brandy, ignite and allow alcohol to burn off. Add wine and 1 quart of the reserved water or enough to cover the shells. Add salt, pepper, onion, bay leaf, thyme, and half the garlic; simmer for 45 minutes.

While shells simmer, in another pot melt the remaining butter and then add the lobster meat. Sautée for 3 minutes, add flour, stirring constantly. Add parsley, green onions, and remaining garlic; cook 5 minutes, or until vegetables are tender. Strain broth from shells through a fine mesh sieve lined with cheesecloth. Add broth to lobster meat. If necessary, add reserved water to give you 3 cups soup; add cream and heat through. Season with salt and pepper to taste.

Serves 4

POTATO LEEK SOUP

Recipe courtesy of Stacey Meyer.

2   tablespoons olive oil
1   onion, diced
2   leeks, sliced
1   stalk celery, sliced
2   cloves garlic, sliced
2   potatoes, diced
1   bay leaf
2   sprigs thyme
1   sprig oregano
5   black peppercorns
1   quart chicken stock
1   cup heavy cream
3/4 cup to 1 cup smoked speckled trout
    Chive blossoms, for garnishing

In a large saucepan, heat the olive oil and then sautée onion, leeks, and celery for 4 to 6 minutes. Add garlic and potatoes. Wrap in cheese cloth the bay leaf, thyme, oregano, and peppercorns. Add to the pan along with the chicken stock; cook until the potatoes are tender, about 35 to 40 minutes. Remove from heat and remove the cheesecloth. Purée mixture in small batches in a blender or food processor until just blended, then add cream. Bring back to a simmer and cook for 5 to 10 minutes more.

To serve, divide the trout equally between each bowls; ladle the soup over top and garnish with chive blossoms.

Serves 4 to 6

Untitled painting, *by Dusti Bonge, courtesy Bonge Foundation.*

LADY CREAM PEA, ANDOUILLE SAUSAGE AND KALE SOUP

Recipe courtesy of Chef Greg Picolo from Bistro at the Maison de Ville.

2   pounds Lady cream peas, dry (black-eyed peas may be substituted)
6   tablespoons olive oil, divided
2   pounds andouille sausage, diced
4   onions, finely diced
2   red bell peppers, finely diced
6   stalks celery, finely diced
3   tablespoons minced garlic
12   quarts chicken stock
8   sprigs marjoram
6   sprigs thyme
4   tablespoons Worcestershire sauce
    Salt and pepper to taste
2   bunches kale, cut into fine strips

Soak peas for at least 1 hour or up to 24 hours.

In a medium sautée pan, heat 3 tablespoons olive oil, add the andouille sausage and cook until lightly brown, about 3 to 5 minutes. Remove the meat from the pan and set aside.

If necessary, add more oil to the pan and then add the onions, bell peppers, and celery; cook until tender, about 3 minutes. Add the garlic, chicken stock, herbs, and peas. Cook over medium heat for 1 hour. Season with Worcestershire sauce, salt, and pepper. Continue to cook the peas until nearly tender. Add the andouille sausage and continue cooking until peas are very tender. Add the kale and cook an additional 3 minutes.

Serve with Gueydan rice—a special rice from Louisiana that tastes and smells like buttered popcorn and can be found in specialty markets.

Serves 6 to 8

Early Spring Rain Near the Levee, *by Rolland Golden, courtesy Rolland Golden.*

Entrées

DUCK AND ANDOUILLE SAUSAGE ÉTOUFFÉE

Recipe courtesy of Ken Smith.

1/2 cup vegetable oil

1/2 cup all-purpose flour

4 cups andouille sausage or smoked sausage

1 cup finely chopped celery

1 cup finely chopped onion

2 cloves garlic, minced

1/2 cup finely chopped red bell pepper

1/2 cup finely chopped green bell pepper

8 cups rich duck or chicken stock

2 tablespoons tomato paste

2 teaspoons dried thyme

3 bay leaves

2 teaspoons salt

1/2 teaspoon black pepper

Cayenne pepper to taste

5 cups chopped roasted duck (or chicken if duck isn't available)

1/4 cup fresh chopped parsley, to garnish

In a cast-iron Dutch oven, heat oil and whisk in flour over medium heat. Whisk until mixture is very dark brown. Reduce heat to low and then add sausage, celery, onion, garlic, and bell peppers; stir to mix well. Add stock 1 cup at a time, stirring well after each addition. Add tomato paste, thyme, bay leaves, salt, black pepper, and cayenne pepper. Raise heat to medium-high and simmer uncovered for 30 minutes, stirring occasionally. Add meat and stir well. Simmer until heated through, about 30 minutes; serve, if desired over rice or pasta. Garnish with the parsley.

Serves 4

Owl Farm, by John Alexander, courtesy Arthur Roger Gallery.

Sea Gulls Plate Design, *by Dusti Bonge, courtesy Bonge Foundation.*

Coq au Vin Blanc

Recipe courtesy of Bob Iacavone.

1 cup olive oil
2 pounds chicken thigh meat, trimmed
   of excess fat
1 white onion, diced
2 stalks celery, diced
1 carrot, peeled and diced
4 cloves garlic, chopped
3/4 cup all-purpose flour
1 bottle (750 mL) white wine
1 cup Madeira
1 cup sherry vinegar
8 cups chicken stock
1 bunch fresh thyme, picked and chopped
   Salt and pepper to taste

In a large pot, heat the oil over medium heat. Add the chicken thighs and cook for 10 to 15 minutes, or until cooked through; remove from the oil.

Add the onion, celery, carrot, and garlic to the oil and cook until slightly brown; stirring often. Cook for 8 to 10 minutes, or until the vegetables are brown. Add the flour and cook for another 5 minutes. Add the wine, Madeira, and sherry vinegar and bring to a boil. Lower the heat and simmer for 6 to 8 minutes. Add the chicken stock and return to a boil. Lower the heat again and simmer until fairly thick. Add the thyme; adjust the seasoning and then stir in the chicken. Serve over rice or accompanied by mashed potatoes.

Serves 4

TROUT MEUNIÈRE AMANDINE

Recipe courtesy of Brian Landry, Executive Chef Galatoire's Restaurant, from Galatoire's: Biography of a Bistro *by Marda Burton and Kenneth Holditch (Hill Street Press).*

3 cups sliced almonds

2 large eggs

1 pint whole milk
   Salt and freshly ground black pepper
      to taste

6 Speckled Trout fillets (7 to 8 ounces each),
      cleaned and boned

2 cups all-purpose flour

1 gallon vegetable oil
   Meunière Butter (see below)

3 medium lemons, cut into wedges

MEUNIÈRE BUTTER

1 pound salted butter

1 tablespoon fresh lemon juice

1 tablespoon red wine vinegar

Preheat the oven to 300 degrees.

Place the almonds in a pan and toast them in the oven for 15 to 20 minutes, stirring every 5 minutes. When the almonds become a light golden brown, remove from the oven and set aside.

Make a wash by whisking together the eggs and milk. Season with salt and pepper. Season the trout with salt and pepper and then dust with flour. Submerge the floured trout in the egg wash. Gently remove the fillets from the egg wash and allow the excess to drip off. Put the fillets back into the flour, then gently shake off the excess flour.

In a large, heavy-bottomed pot, heat the oil to 350 degrees. Test the readiness of the oil by sprinkling a pinch of flour over it. The flour will brown instantly when the oil has reached the correct temperature. Add the trout and fry for 4 to 5 minutes. Remove the fish when the crust is golden brown. Top each fried trout fillet with almonds and warmed Meunière Butter. Garnish with lemon wedges and serve at once.

Recipe continued on page 144

Untitled Work on Paper, *by Dusti Bonge, courtesy Bonge Foundation.*

To make the Meunière Butter, heat a medium saucepan over medium heat. Melt the butter, whisking constantly, for 8 to 10 minutes, until the sediment (milk solids) in the butter turn dark brown, almost (but not quite) to the point of burning, and the liquid is a deep golden brown color. Remove the pan from the heat and continue to whisk slowly, adding the lemon juice and vinegar to the browned butter. The sauce will froth until the liquids have evaporated. When the frothing subsides, the sauce is complete.

Serves 6

Untitled Work on Paper, *by Dusti Bonge, courtesy Bonge Foundation.*

River Parish Fall "Grillades"

Recipe courtesy of Winifred Berthelot Gilbert.

1/2 cup butter
1/2 cup flour
1 large onion, diced
1/4 cup diced green bell pepper
1/2 bunch green onions, chopped
1/2 cup chopped parsley
8 turnips diced (about 3 to 4 pounds)
1 quart beef broth
4 sirloin tip rounds (3 pounds tenderized)
2 tablespoons olive oil
Salt and pepper to taste
Crushed red pepper to taste

In a large Dutch oven, melt butter and add flour. Cook to a dark roux, about 15 to 20 minutes (mixture should smell nutty and be a dark brown). Add onion, bell pepper, green onions, and parsley; cook for 5 to 6 minutes while stirring. Add a little water so as not to burn roux. Add the turnips and the beef broth. In a sautée pan, brown the sirloin in the olive oil. Add the sirloin to the Dutch oven and season with salt and both peppers. Bring to a boil, then turn down to a simmer; cook for 1 hour or until the beef is very tender and falling apart. If necessary, add more water or broth.

Serves 4 to 6

TURKEY JAMBALAYA

Recipe courtesy of Jack Leonardi from Jacque-Imo's.

4	tablespoons unsalted butter
2	cups chopped yellow onions
1	cup chopped celery
1	cup chopped green bell peppers
1 1/2	tablespoons minced garlic
1	pound sliced turkey medallions
12	ounces turkey ham, diced
3	teaspoons Poultry Magic Seasoning
1	teaspoon cayenne
2	bay leaves
2 1/2	tablespoons tomato paste
1 3/4	cups peeled and diced tomatoes, with juices
1 3/4	cups chicken stock or canned low-sodium chicken broth
3/4	cup tomato sauce
4	cups cooked white rice
	Chopped green onion, for garnish

In a 6-quart Dutch oven or stockpot over medium heat, melt the butter then add the onions, celery, and bell peppers; cook, stirring until vegetables are soft and starting to color, about 8 to 10 minutes. Add the garlic and cook, stirring, until fragrant and soft, about 2 minutes. Add the turkey, turkey ham, poultry seasoning, cayenne, and bay leaves; cook, stirring, for 30 seconds. Add the tomato paste and stir to incorporate. Add the tomatoes with juices, chicken stock, and tomato sauce; stir well and then bring to a boil, about 3 to 4 minutes. Reduce the heat slightly and simmer, stirring occasionally, until the mixture is thick and reduced by almost half, about 25 to 30 minutes. Add the rice to the sauce and stir well to incorporate; cook, stirring until hot, for another 3 to 5 minutes.

Remove the pot from the heat and adjust the seasoning to taste. Transfer the jambalaya to a large serving bowl or individual plates, garnish with green onions, and serve immediately.

Serves 6 to 8

Deluge, *by Jeff Stoiler, courtesy Jeff Stoiler.*

Oak Tree at Sunset, *by Jason Langley, courtesy Jason Langley.*

LOUISIANA-STYLE CRAWFISH ÉTOUFFÉE

Recipe courtesy of John Folse from The Encyclopedia of Cajun & Creole Cuisine
(Chef John Folse & Company Publishing).

1/4   pound butter
1   cup diced onions
1/2   cup diced celery
1/2   cup diced green bell pepper
1/2   cup diced red bell pepper
1/2   cup diced tomato
2   tablespoons minced garlic
2   bay leaves
1   cup flour
2   pounds crawfish tails, cleaned
1/2   cup tomato sauce
2   quarts crawfish stock or water
2   tablespoons sherry
1   cup sliced green onions
1/2   cup chopped parsley
  Salt and cayenne pepper to taste
2   cups steamed white rice
  Louisiana hot sauce to taste

In a 2-gallon saucepot, melt butter over medium-high heat. Add onions, celery, bell peppers, tomato, garlic, and bay leaves. Sautée 3 to 5 minutes, or until vegetables are wilted. Whisk in flour, stirring constantly until a roux is achieved. Blend crawfish tails and tomato sauce into mixture; cook 5 minutes, stirring to prevent tomato sauce from scorching. Slowly add crawfish stock or water until a sauce-like consistency is achieved; add more stock as necessary to retain consistency. Bring to a rolling boil then reduce to a simmer and cook 30 minutes, stirring occasionally. Add sherry, green onions, and parsley. Cook 5 minutes then season with salt and cayenne pepper. Serve over steamed white rice with a few dashes of hot sauce.

Serves 6

POACHED MUSSELS AND CHORIZO

Recipe courtesy of Kevin Vizard from Vizards on the Avenue.

3 shallots, minced

1 cup diced leeks

1 cup diced fennel

3/4 pound chorizo sausage, sliced into
   1/2-inch-thick pieces

2 tablespoons olive oil

1 cup Tomato Concasse (see below)

1 cup white wine

1/2 cup oyster liquid

1 teaspoon chopped flat-leaf parsley

1/2 teaspoon chopped tarragon

60 to 70 mussels, scrubbed and de-bearded
   Salt and pepper to taste

4 ounces butter

TOMATO CONCASSE

2 large tomatoes

1 teaspoon salt

In a large saucepan, sautée the shallots, leeks, fennel, and chorizo in oil until shallots turn clear. Add the Tomato Concasse, wine, and oyster liquid. Bring to a boil and add herbs and mussels; cook for 6 to 8 minutes, or until mussels open. Discard any mussels that do not open. Evenly divide mussels between four bowls. Season the mussel broth with salt and pepper, add more herbs if necessary, and swirl in butter. Divide sauce evenly among bowls and serve.

For the concasse, bring 1 quart of water and the salt to a boil in a medium saucepan. Score the tomatoes and remove the stems. Drop the tomatoes in the water; as soon as the skins begin to loosen, remove the tomatoes and immediately immerse them in an ice bath. Remove the skin and quarter the tomatoes. Remove the seeds and dice the tomatoes.

Serves 4

On the Edge, Grand Bayou, *by Bobby Wozniak, courtesy LeMieux Galleries.*

Pork Shoulder Roast with Onion Jus and Rice

Recipe courtesy of Donald Link from Herbsaint and Cochon.

2   pounds pork shoulder
    Salt and pepper to taste
1   tablespoon chile flakes
6   cloves garlic, thinly sliced
1   cup flour, divided
1/4 cup olive or canola oil
1   red onion, thinly sliced
2   tablespoons chopped fresh thyme
1   quart chicken stock
4   bay leaves
3   tablespoons lemon juice
1   dash Worcestershire

Three Sisters,
by Amy McKinnon,
courtesy Amy McKinnon.

Season pork generously all over with salt, pepper and chile flakes. Make six 1-inch-deep and -wide cuts all over pork and insert garlic. Lightly coat pork with a little flour and sear over medium-high heat in oil until golden brown; remove and set aside. Sprinkle $1/4$ cup flour into oil remaining in pan and stir until browned. You may need to add about $1/4$ cup more oil. Add the onion and thyme and sautée for 5 minutes. Add chicken stock, pork, bay leaves, lemon juice, and Worcestershire; bake, covered, at 300 degrees for $1^1/2$ to 2 hours, or until tender. To serve, cut pork into desired portions and spoon sauce over it. Serve with white rice.

Serves 4 to 6

Pelican Plate Design, *by Dusti Bonge, courtesy Bonge Foundation.*

SMOKED SAUSAGE AND CREOLE TOMATO JAMBALAYA

Recipe courtesy of John Folse from The Encyclopedia of Cajun & Creole Cuisine
(Chef John Folse & Company Publishing).

1/4 cup vegetable oil
1 cup diced onion
1 cup diced celery
1/2 cup diced red bell pepper
1 tablespoon minced garlic
2 pounds smoked sausage, sliced
2 (8-ounce) cans tomato sauce
1 cup diced tomatoes
3 cups chicken stock or water
3 cups long-grain rice
  Salt and cracked black pepper to taste
  Louisiana hot sauce to taste
1/2 cup sliced green onions
1/4 cup chopped parsley

In a Dutch oven, heat oil over medium-high heat. Sautée onion, celery, bell pepper, and garlic for 3 to 5 minutes, or until vegetables are wilted. Mix in sausage and cook 5 minutes. Blend in tomato sauce, tomatoes, and chicken stock. Bring to a rolling boil, and stir in rice. Return to a boil, then reduce heat to low. Season with salt, pepper, and hot sauce. Cover pot and cook. Do not stir or remove lid for 20 minutes. Remove lid, add green onions and parsley. Stir mixture once to make sure that the rice is not sticking and scorching. Cover and cook 10 to 15 minutes more. Remove from heat and allow to steam 15 minutes before serving.

Note: The original jambalaya of New Orleans was tomato-based and flavored with a combination of sausages, ham, and chicken. Often, the dish was "thrown together" at a moment's notice when unexpected friends dropped by and a quick entrée was needed. In such a case, sometimes heavy smoked sausage and tomatoes were the only ingredients needed for a great spur-of-the-moment lunch.

Serves 6

SAUTÉED CATFISH WITH LOUISIANA SHRIMP AND JALAPEÑO SLAW

Recipe courtesy of Donald Link from Herbsaint and Cochon.

1 cup all-purpose flour
1 cup white cornmeal
4 to 6 (6-ounce) catfish fillets
　Salt and pepper to taste
1 teaspoon cayenne pepper
1/4 cup vegetable oil

SLAW

1 cup mirliton, cut into matchsticks
　(also known as chayote)
1 cup kohlrabi, cut into matchsticks
1 cup julienned scallions
1 cup julienned fresh turnips
1 cup chopped spinach
1 pound boiled shrimp

DRESSING

2 tablespoons jalapeño, minced and seeded
2 tablespoons red wine vinegar
1 tablespoon lemon juice
1 teaspoon Dijon mustard
1 teaspoon chopped capers
1 egg yolk
　Salt and pepper to taste
　Cayenne pepper to taste
1 cup vegetable oil

Mix flour and cornmeal together; season catfish with salt, black pepper, and cayenne, coat with the flour mixture.

In a large sautée pan, heat oil over medium high heat and cook catfish for about 4 minutes on each side.

For the slaw, combine the vegetables in a medium mixing bowl. Chop up the boiled shrimp and combine with the vegetables.

For the dressing, mix everything together except the oil. Slowly add the oil in a slow, steady stream to form an emulsion. Combine the dressing with the slaw.

Divide the slaw between four plates. Top the with the catfish.

Serves 4

BRAISED GREENS WITH BACON AND ONIONS

Recipe courtesy of Corbin Evans from Savvy Gourmet.

3   medium yellow onions, peeled and sliced
1   cup bacon fat
1   to 2 cups chicken stock or water
2   tablespoons brown sugar
1/4 cup cider vinegar
1/2 tablespoon dried red pepper flakes
4   pounds greens, trimmed, washed well,
    and rough chopped (turnip, collard,
    mustard, kale, chard, escarole, etc.)
    Kosher salt and freshly ground black
    pepper to taste
2   tablespoons Creole mustard

In a large sautée or saucepan over medium-high heat, sweat onions in bacon fat. Add remaining ingredients, except greens, seasonings, and mustard, and stir to dissolve sugar. Add half of the greens and stir until wilted down, then add remaining greens and season with salt and pepper. Lower heat and let cook 35 to 45 minutes, or until tender. When ready to serve, stir in Creole mustard and adjust seasoning.

Serves 4

SNAPPER ANTHONY

Recipe courtesy of Kevin Vizard from Vizards on the Avenue.

1 1/4 cups white wine, divided
1 cup plus 2 tablespoons olive oil, divided
1 bunch thyme
2 sprigs rosemary
1 bay leaf
2 fennel bulbs, sliced
2 large leeks, sliced
2 artichoke hearts, leaves removed, cleaned, and sliced
2 (7-ounce) snapper fillets
1 teaspoon salt
1 teaspoon pepper
1/2 shallot, finely diced
1 cup diced tomatoes
2 tablespoons chopped tarragon
4 tablespoons unsalted butter

In a sautée pan with high sides, combine 1 cup white wine, 1 cup olive oil, thyme, rosemary, and bay leaf. Add the fennel and gently bring to a simmer. Cook until the fennel is tender, remove with a slotted spoon and set aside. Using the same technique, cook the leeks and then the artichokes, one at a time. When all vegetables are cooked, return to the same pan and keep on low heat while cooking fish.

In a medium sautée pan, heat remaining olive oil over medium-high heat. Season snapper with salt and pepper and sear 2 minutes on each side. Remove fish and keep warm.

Deglaze pan with remaining wine, add shallot and then cook until translucent. Add tomatoes and reduce liquid by half. Taste for salt and pepper. Finish sauce with tarragon and butter, swirling the pan until all butter is incorporated.

To serve, divide vegetables evenly among four plates, place snapper on top of vegetables and then spoon sauce over fish.

Serves 4

Untitled Kitchens and Dining Rooms, *by Robert Brantley, courtesy Robert Brantley.*

TURKEY MIGNONS WITH RASPBERRY HOT PEPPER SAUCE

Recipe courtesy of Jack Leonardi of Jacques-Imos and Crabby Jack.

4 turkey mignons
2 teaspoons Poultry Magic Seasoning
2 teaspoons olive oil
   Raspberry Hot Pepper Sauce (see below)
   Mashed Sweet Potatoes (see right)

RASPBERRY HOT PEPPER SAUCE

1 cup Blackberry Patch raspberry syrup or
   other raspberry syrup
1 cup hot pepper jelly
1/4 teaspoon cornstarch
1/2 teaspoon water

MASHED SWEET POTATOES

2 pounds sweet potatoes, peeled and
   cut into 1-inch pieces
3/4 cup half-and-half
6 tablespoons light brown sugar
1/8 teaspoon salt
   Pecans, chopped and toasted, for garnish

Season both sides of the mignons with the poultry seasoning.

In a large sautée pan over medium-high heat, heat the oil until hot, but not smoking. Add the mignons and stir, 2 to 3 minutes. Reduce the heat to medium, turn the medallions and cook the other side until cooked through, about 4 to 5 minutes.

Place one mignon on each of four large plates, drizzle with the Raspberry Hot Pepper Sauce and some Mashed Sweet Potatoes. Serve immediately.

For the sauce, combine the syrup and pepper jelly in a small saucepan and place over medium heat.

Combine the cornstarch and water in a small bowl to make a paste and then add to the syrup mixture. Bring to a slow boil and then cook until thick and well combined, about 3 minutes. Remove from heat and let cool slightly before serving.

For the potatoes, place the potatoes in a medium pot, cover with water and boil until tender, about 15 minutes. Drain well in a colander and transfer to a large bowl.

Add half-and-half, brown sugar, and salt; beat on high speed with an electric mixer, or mash by hand until smooth. Cover to keep warm. Garnish the top of each serving with chopped pecans and serve.

Serves 4

Ponchartrain Piers, *by Jason Langley, courtesy Jason Langley.*

SHRIMP AND CREOLE TOMATO SAUCE

Recipe courtesy of Kevin Vizard from Vizards on the Avenue.

2 tablespoons olive oil
1 1/2 cups chopped yellow onions
1 cup chopped celery
1 cup chopped bell pepper
1 tablespoon chopped garlic
6 cups chopped Creole tomatoes
1 cup shrimp stock
1 bay leaf
1 teaspoon chopped fresh thyme
2 pounds jumbo shrimp (use heads and shells for shrimp stock)
1 lemon, juiced
1 tablespoon chopped fresh basil
1/2 teaspoon Tabasco sauce
1 teaspoon red pepper flakes
Salt and pepper to taste
2 tablespoons chopped parsley, to garnish

In large sautée pan, heat oil over medium-high heat; add onions, celery, bell pepper, and garlic and cook until vegetables are very tender. Make sure to lower heat so you don't burn the garlic. Add tomatoes, shrimp stock, bay leaf, and thyme and cook until liquid is reduced by half. Add shrimp, lemon juice, basil, Tabasco, red pepper flakes, salt, and pepper and continue cooking for 5 to 10 minutes, making sure to not boil the sauce. (It should never go above a simmer so as not to toughen the shrimp). Taste for seasoning and serve over steamed rice. Garnish with parsley and a little bit of green onion if desired.

Serves 4

Untitled Kitchens and Dining Rooms, *by Robert Brantley, courtesy Robert Brantley.*

VENISON DENVER LEG WITH CHANTERELLES, WATERCRESS, AND TARRAGON BEURRE NOISETTE

Recipe courtesy of Chuck Subra from La Côte Brasserie.

20 ounces venison Denver leg or venison loin*
3/4 cup olive oil, divided
1 1/2 tablespoons minced garlic, divided
1 tablespoon chopped thyme
1 tablespoon chopped basil
2 pounds chanterelle mushrooms
8 ounces watercress
1/2 pound butter
Sea salt and black pepper to taste
2 ounces tarragon, chopped (about 1 bunch)

* Venison can be ordered online from D'artagnan.

Clean all the venison of all fat and silver skin. In a medium mixing bowl, combine 1/2 cup olive oil, 1 tablespoon garlic, thyme, and basil; mix well. Place the venison in the marinade and let sit for 1 hour. Meanwhile, clean the mushrooms and pick the stems from the watercress.

Heat a large sautée pan over medium-high heat; add remaining olive oil. Remove the venison from the marinade and season with sea salt and black pepper. Place venison in the pan, browning on each side and cook until desired temperature, about 7 minutes for medium rare. Remove the venison from the skillet and let rest for 3 to 5 minutes.

Add the mushrooms and remaining garlic to the pan, cook for 3 minutes, or until the mushrooms are tender. Add the watercress and cook until lightly wilted. Season to taste with sea salt and pepper. Remove from the heat and keep warm.

Recipe continued on page 166

Untitled painting, *by Dusti Bonge, courtesy Bonge Foundation.*

In a medium sautée pan over medium-high heat, add butter, sea salt and black pepper. Let the butter start to brown lightly. Add the tarragon and remove from heat. Check for correct seasoning.

To serve, place the mushroom and watercress mixture in the center of a dinner plate. Thinly slice the venison and fan it around the mushroom mixture. Using a sauce spoon, gently drizzle the tarragon beurre noisette around and over the venison.

Serves 6

Helicopter Hands, *by Rolland Golden, courtesy Rolland Golden.*

Roast Chicken Au Jus with Lemon and Basil

Recipe courtesy of Donald Link from Herbsaint and Cochon.

1 (3- to 4-pound) whole free-range chicken
  Salt and freshly ground pepper
  Pinch paprika
6 fresh basil leaves
4 thin slices lemon (round)
1 clove garlic, thinly sliced
1 onion, sliced into 1/2-inch rounds
1 cup white wine
1 cup water
2 tablespoons butter

Preheat oven to 350 degrees.

Thoroughly rinse and dry off chicken, removing all excess moisture; season generously with salt, pepper, and paprika. Use half the volume of paprika as salt and pepper.

Place the basil, lemon slices, and garlic under the skin of the chicken. Distribute equal amounts on both sides of the chicken. Place a basil leaf and a lemon slice near the thighs as well.

Place the onion on a lightly oiled roasting pan and place the chicken on top, breast side up.

Bake chicken for about 40 minutes; ovens may vary, so use your judgment. When chicken is cooked, remove it from the roasting pan and place on a rack or plate to sit.

Pour the wine onto the hot roasting pan and scrape the pan. When the wine is half gone, add the water and then let liquid reduce by half. Add butter to melt and then set aside.

Carefully remove the parts of the chicken with a sharp knife and keep the skin attached. (This may take some practice.) Serve with the pan sauce.

Serves 4

River Road Oak, *by Kate Trepagnier, courtesy LeMieux Galleries.*

COMMUNITY COFFEE–CURED PORK CHOP WITH SWEET POTATO GNOCCHI AND CEDAR-SMOKED TOMATO PURÉE

Recipe courtesy of Chuck Subra from La Côte Brasserie.

BRINE

- 1 quart apple cider
- 5 quarts water
- 1 cup brown sugar
- 1 cup Community Coffee (dark roast) or other strong roast
- 1 tablespoon whole black peppercorns
- 3 tablespoons fresh thyme
- 4 (10-ounce) pork chops

SWEET POTATO GNOCCHI

- 2 pounds sweet potatoes
- 3 tablespoons butter, melted
- 1/8 teaspoon nutmeg
- 1 tablespoon olive oil
  Pepper, to taste
- 1 cup all-purpose flour
  Salt

CEDAR-SMOKED TOMATO PURÉE

- 5 tomatoes
- 1/2 cup cedar wood chips
- 1 tablespoon olive oil
- 1 onion, diced
- 1 tablespoon minced garlic
- 1 cup chicken stock
- 1 tablespoon chopped fresh thyme
- 1 tablespoon chopped fresh basil
  Salt and pepper to taste

For the brine, combine all ingredients except pork chops in a large nonreactive pot and bring to a simmer; remove from the heat and cool in an ice bath. Pour cooled liquid over the pork chops and then place in the refrigerator for 24 hours.

For the gnocchi, preheat oven to 375 degrees. Place potatoes in a sheetpan and roast for 1 to 1 1/2 hours or until cooked through. Remove from oven and let cool until room temperature. Peel and run through a potato ricer. Gently fold in the butter, nutmeg, olive oil, and pepper. Once everything is combined, gently fold in the flour in small increments until the dough begins to come together. It should be neither too sticky nor too dry. The dough should have a light consistency. If you work it too hard, the gnocchi will be tough and chewy. Roll the dough into a log before resting. Let the batter rest for 30 minutes. Fill an 8-quart saucepot

Recipe continued on next page

half full with water. Salt the water and bring to a simmer. Fill a pastry bag with the dough and pipe the dough into the water, cutting the dough into ¼-inch pieces. (If a pastry bag is not available, use 2 teaspoons and scoop small portions into the simmering water.) Let the gnocchi cook for approximately 3 minutes.

Remove from the water and place into an ice bath to stop the cooking process. Remove the gnocchi from the ice bath, drain well and drizzle lightly with water; place in the refrigerator.

For the purée, blanch, peel, and halve the tomatoes. Smoke them according to the directions in a stove-top smoker using the cedar chips for 1 hour. Place a medium saucepot over medium-heat, add the olive oil and cook the onion until translucent. Add the garlic and cook for 1 minute. Add the smoked tomatoes and chicken stock. Bring to a simmer. Cook for 10 minutes then add the thyme and basil. Cook for 10 minutes more and then purée in a food processor. Strain the sauce, season to taste with salt and pepper; keep hot.

Remove the pork chops from the brine solution and wash off the coffee and other particles remaining. (If the pork chops are not washed, the particles will burn when grilling.) Season the pork chops with salt and pepper and then grill over medium heat until cooked to about medium or desired temperature of doneness.

In a large skillet, brown 2 tablespoons of butter. Gently add gnocchi and heat through. Season with salt and pepper. Place the gnocchi in the center of the serving dish. Place the pork chop on top of the gnocchi. Spoon the sauce around the chop, the gnocchi, and then lightly over the pork chop. Garnish with fresh herbs and serve.

Serves 4

Reeds Mandeville Lakefront, *by Jason Langley, courtesy Jason Langley.*

GLAZED KING SALMON WITH TABASCO AND STEEN'S CANE SYRUP, ROASTED MIRLITON SHRIMP RAGOUT

Recipe courtesy of Chuck Subra from La Côte Brasserie.

4 each mirliton or chayote, peeled,
    cored, and diced
1 onion, diced small
2 stalks celery, diced small
2 tablespoons minced garlic
2 tablespoons chopped fresh thyme
1 pound (70/90 count) shrimp
1/4 cup white wine
1 cup chicken stock
1/2 cup panko breadcrumbs (regular
    can be substituted)
1/4 cup grated Parmesan cheese
1 tablespoon Tabasco sauce
2 tablespoons Steen's Cane Syrup*
3 tablespoons olive oil
6 (6-ounce) King salmon fillets
    Sea salt and black pepper to taste

BEURRE BLANC
1/4 cup champagne vinegar
1 cup white wine
1 bay leaf
2 tablespoons chopped shallots or onion
2 whole black peppercorns
4 tablespoons heavy cream
1/2 pound butter (unsalted)
1 teaspoon lemon juice
    Sea salt to taste

Preheat oven to 350 degrees.

Steam or boil the mirliton for 5 minutes; remove and chill. In a medium saucepan, cook onion, celery, and garlic over medium heat until golden. Add cooked mirliton, thyme, and shrimp. Deglaze with wine and then reduce by half. Add stock and bring to a boil. Add the breadcrumbs until desired consistency. It should have the consistency of a thick sauce and should be able to coat the back of a spoon. Add half of the cheese. Place the mixture into a baking pan and cover with remaining cheese. Brown in oven for 10 to 15 minutes; reserve and keep warm.

In a small mixing bowl, combine the Tabasco and cane syrup together; mix thoroughly.

In a large sautée pan over medium to high heat, add the olive oil. Season the salmon with sea salt and black pepper. Place the salmon in the skillet

Recipe continued on page 174

* Syrup can be ordered online.

On Ice, *by Amy McKinnon, courtesy Amy McKinnon.*

Flora Path II, *by Deedra D. Ludwig, courtesy LeMieux Galleries.*

and cook until desired temperature, 140 degrees for medium-rare and 125 degrees for rare, turning half way through the cooking process. Once the salmon is cooked, spoon the glaze over top. To serve, place the mirliton ragout in the center of a dinner plate or bowl, place the salmon on top and drizzle with the Beurre Blanc.

To make the Beurre Blanc, place a small saucepan over medium to high heat. Add the vinegar, wine, bay leaf, shallots, and black peppercorns. Reduce until approximately 1 tablespoon of liquid remains. Add heavy cream and then reduce by half; remove from heat. Using a whisk add the butter, 1 tablespoon at a time, until the butter is melted. Do not add more until all the butter is melted. (Adding the butter too fast will cause the sauce to break). Add the lemon juice and season to taste with the salt. Strain and keep in a warm place.

Serves 6

Roast Pork Latino-Style

Recipe courtesy of Adolfo Garcia from RioMar and La Boca.

MOJO

- 1 cup pomace olive oil or extra virgin olive oil
- 10 cloves garlic
- 1 whole orange, peeled, seeded, and quartered
- 2 limes, juiced
- 3 tablespoons whole oregano
- 2 teaspoons ground cumin
- 2 cups water
- 4 tablespoons salt

- 1 bone-in pork butt

Preheat oven to 375 degrees.

Put all mojo ingredients into a blender until smooth. Add more water if needed. Rub pork butt with mojo and then bake in oven, covered, for 5 hours. The pork will fall off the bone and is best served with rice and beans.

Serves 4 to 6

China Setting III, *by Patricia Pilie, courtesy Carol Robinson Gallery.*

KOBE BEEF SHORT RIBS WITH
WILD RICE PILAF AND SAUCE BORDELAISE

Recipe courtesy of Tom Wolfe from Peristyle.

10 pounds Kobe beef short ribs
    Kosher salt
    Freshly ground black pepper
    Creole spice
    Canola oil
3 carrots, peeled and diced
4 cloves garlic, smashed
1 1/2 large onions, peeled and large dice
3 stalks celery, large dice
1/4 cup tomato paste
1 bottle (750 mL) red wine
1 gallon beef stock
2 bay leaves
2 sprigs thyme and 1/4 cup picked
    thyme leaves
1 sprig rosemary

WILD RICE PILAF

1 cup diced yellow onions
1/2 cup diced celery
1/2 cup small dice carrot
2 bay leaves
1 tablespoon minced garlic
2 tablespoons Plugra butter
2 pounds clean wild rice
3 quarts chicken stock
    Salt and pepper to taste

SAUCE BORDELAISE

1 cup diced onion
2 sprigs thyme
2 cloves garlic, smashed
2 bay leaves
1 bottle (750 ML) red wine
1 cup red wine vinegar
1 1/2 quarts demi-glace (can be bought
    at specialty shops)
1 1/2 quarts chicken stock

Score the ribs diagonally on meat side about
1/16-inch deep. Season with salt, pepper, Creole
spice and a little oil. Sear on grill on both sides.

In a large sautée pan with high sides, caramelize
carrots, garlic, onion, and celery. Add tomato
paste and caramelize. Add wine and reduce by
half. Add beef stock, check flavor, and submerge
short ribs. Add the bay leaves, thyme, rosemary,
and cover tightly and braise at 350 degrees for
about 3 hours or until ribs are fork tender.
Remove short ribs to cool. Skim fat from the
braising liquid.

For the rice, in a medium pot, sweat the onion, celery, carrot, bay leaves, and garlic in the butter until the vegetables become soft. Add the wild rice and stock and cover the pot and bring to a slow simmer. Cook rice until it has "popped." Once cooked, spread the rice out on a sheetpan and allow to cool. Store in a plastic container. Or serve immediately and any extra can be cooled and stored in a plastic container.

For the sauce, in a large saucepan, cook onion until tender, about 5 minutes; add thyme, garlic, bay leaves, red wine, and red wine vinegar. Reduce until $1/4$ of the liquid is left. Add demi-glace and chicken stock and reduce slowly until approximately $1^{1}/_{2}$ quarts, about 1 hour (place into a water bath to cool). You will have extra sauce– it can be frozen in small containers for later use.

Reheat in small batches and finish with lemon juice to taste and chopped fresh parsley. In shallow bowls, place $1/_{2}$ to $3/_{4}$ cup rice. To serve, divide the short ribs equally among the bowls. Ladle $1/_{4}$ cup sauce, or more if desired, over the ribs. Garnish with fresh thyme leaves.

Serves 8 to 10

American Queen in Morning Fog, *by Karl Kratzberg, courtesy A.G. Wagner Studio.*

PAN-SEARED CHICKEN BREAST ON BBQ CHICKEN POTATO HASH WITH OVEN-ROASTED TOMATOES AND LEMON BRANDY GASTRIQUE

Recipe courtesy of Tom Wolfe from Peristyle.

2 (3- to 4-pound) whole free-range chickens
   Kosher salt and coarse black pepper
    to taste
1 bunch fresh thyme
2 bay leaves
2 heads garlic, cut in half

OVEN-ROASTED TOMATOES
6 Roma tomatoes
   Salt and coarsely ground pepper
    to taste

BBQ CHICKEN POTATO HASH
1/4 cup chicken fat
1 1/2 cups diced potatoes
3 tablespoons butter
1/2 cup diced onions
2 teaspoons chopped garlic
1/4 cup diced tomato
3 tablespoons diced green bell pepper
1 cup shredded chicken confit
3 tablespoons BBQ sauce
2 tablespoons chicken stock to moisten
1 tablespoon chopped parsley
   Kosher salt and black pepper to taste

LEMON BRANDY GASTRIQUE
1 bottle (1 liter) brandy
2 cups sugar
4 tablespoons water
1 cup apple cider vinegar
1/2 cup chopped lemon segments

Butcher chickens by de-boning and separating the breast from the leg quarter. The leg quarters will be used for the chicken confit for the BBQ Chicken Potato Hash. The breasts will be sautéed just before putting the dish together.

Cover chicken leg quarters with duck fat, pork fat or olive oil. Place in a preheated oven at 250 degrees for 3 1/2 hours, or until falling off the bone. Remove from fat, de-bone and shred chicken leg meat.

To make the oven-dried tomatoes, cut tomatoes into quarters. Place tomato quarters skin-side down on a sheetpan with parchment paper and then season with salt and pepper. Place in a pre-heated oven at 250 degrees for 2 hours.

Note: You can cook the tomatoes in the same oven as the chicken confit, as the oven is at the same temperature.

To make the hash, heat the chicken fat and fry the diced potatoes in a sautée pan with high sides for approximately 4 minutes until golden brown.

In a large sautée pan, melt butter and sautée onions, garlic, tomato, and bell pepper; cook until tender, about 3 to 5 minutes. Add the chicken confit and cook for 2 minutes longer. Add the potatoes, BBQ sauce and chicken stock; cook for 4 to 5 minutes. Add chopped parsley, salt, and pepper.

For the gastrique, in a small nonreactive saucepan over medium-high heat, bring the brandy to a boil and reduce to 1 cup.

In another saucepan, combine the sugar and water and cook over medium to low heat without stirring for approximately 3 to 5 minutes, or until the sugar is completely melted and caramelized. When the sugar begins to caramelize, swirl the pan to even out the color.

Pull off the heat and slowly add the vinegar to the sugar mixture. The mixture will bubble. Return to heat and whisk constantly until well blended. Add the brandy reduction and lemon segments. Simmer the mix until it comes to approximately 2 cups.

To finish, season and sautée the chicken for 4 to 5 minutes on each side, or until the internal temperature reaches 165 degrees F. Place the chicken breast on top of the BBQ Chicken Potato Hash. Serve with the Oven-Dried Tomatoes and the Lemon Brandy Gastrique.

Serves 4 to 6

Desserts

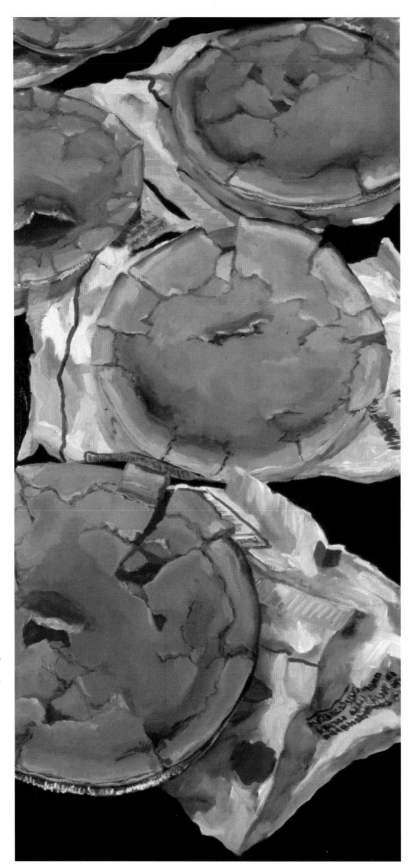

Hubigs, by Amy McKinnon,
courtesy Amy McKinnon.

CHOCOLATE POTS DE CRÈME

Courtesy of Mary Ann Meyer.

2 cups heavy cream

1/4 cup sugar

6 egg yolks

4 ounces semisweet chocolate, melted

1 tablespoon vanilla extract

Preheat oven to 325 degrees.

In a small saucepan, combine cream and sugar and scald.

In a small bowl, beat egg yolks until light and creamy; add to cream, stirring constantly. Add melted chocolate and vanilla, and then pour mixture into six small ramekins. Set ramekins in pan with sides filled with enough hot water to go part way up the ramekins. Cover the pan with aluminum foil and then bake for 20 minutes; refrigerate until ready to serve. Serve at room temperature.

Serves 6

CREOLE CREAM CHEESE

Recipe courtesy of Poppy Tooker from Savvy Gourmet and Slow Food New Orleans.

1/2 gallon skim milk
6 to 8 drops liquid vegetable rennet
1/4 tablespoon salt

Mix the milk, rennet, and salt together in a big glass or a stainless-steel bowl. Cover loosely with plastic wrap and leave out at room temperature for 24 hours.

After 24 hours, there will be a large single curd floating in whey. With a slotted spoon, spoon pieces of the large curd into pint-size cheese molds. (Poppy uses plastic pint containers that she has dotted with holes using a soldering iron.)

Put molds on a rack in a pan, cover loosely with plastic wrap and allow to drain while refrigerated for 8 hours. Turn cheeses out of the molds and store in covered containers for up to 2 weeks.

Note: Creole cream cheese is usually eaten by covering with a small amount of cream and sprinkling with sugar for breakfast. Or also, it is eaten savory style with salt and pepper.

Serves 4

FROZEN CREOLE CREAM CHEESE

Recipe courtesy of Poppy Tooker from Savvy Gourmet and Slow Food New Orleans.

4 pints Creole Cream Cheese (see
  page 184)
1 cup sugar
2 teaspoons vanilla extract
1 cup heavy cream

Blend all ingredients together until smooth. Using an ice cream maker, freeze according to the manufacturer's directions and freeze to soft serve consistency, then serve.

Serves 8 (yields 2 quarts)

City Park Soliloquy, *by Albert Wagner, courtesy A.G. Wagner Studio and Gallery.*

CALAS

Recipe courtesy of Poppy Tooker from Savvy Gourmet and Slow Food New Orleans.

2 cups cooked rice
6 tablespoons flour
3 heaping tablespoons sugar
2 teaspoons baking powder
1/4 teaspoon salt
2 eggs
4 teaspoons vanilla
  Nutmeg
  Powdered sugar

Mix the rice and dry ingredients together thoroughly. Add the eggs and vanilla and, when thoroughly mixed, drop by spoonfuls into 360-degree deep fat and fry until brown. Drain on paper towels. Sprinkle with powdered sugar and serve hot.

Note: Maintain mixture below 70 degrees or separation will occur when dropped into the hot oil.

Serves 6 (yields approximately 12 calas)

Vase, by John Hodge, *courtesy John Hodge.*

TURTLES

Recipe courtesy of Mary Ann Meyer.

1 tablespoon butter, softened
1 pound pecans
1 pound caramels
2 tablespoons water
8 ounces semisweet chocolate

Spread butter on a baking sheet and then lay nuts over top. Melt caramels in a double boiler with the water. Drop 1 teaspoon melted caramel over each pecan. When cool, lift each nut off of the pan and then place on buttered tin foil. Melt chocolate in microwave and then spread over each nut; cool.

Note: You may cluster the nuts together for larger turtles.

Serves 10 to 12

Untitled, Two Women,
by Paul Ninas, courtesy
LeMieux Galleries.

The New Forest, *by Deedra D. Ludwig, courtesy LeMieux Galleries.*

WHITE CHOCOLATE BREAD PUDDING

Recipe courtesy of John Folse from The Encyclopedia of Cajun & Creole Cuisine
(Chef John Folse & Company Publishing).

4   eggs
6   egg yolks
4   cups heavy whipping cream
1   cup milk
1   cup sugar
9   ounces white chocolate
3   (10-inch) loaves French bread, cut
    into 1/2-inch-thick slices

In a large mixing bowl, whisk together eggs and egg yolks; set aside.

In a large saucepan, combine cream, milk, and sugar. Bring mixture to a low simmer then add the white chocolate. Whisk until chocolate is completely melted. Remove pot from heat and quickly stir in eggs. Blend thoroughly to keep eggs from scrambling.

In a 9 x 13-inch baking dish, place bread slices to make two to three layers. Pour half of the cream mixture over bread. Press bread gently allowing cream mixture to be absorbed evenly into bread. Once most of mixture has been soaked up, pour remaining cream over bread and press gently. Cover dish with foil and let soak a minimum of 5 hours prior to baking.

Preheat oven to 300 degrees. Bake, covered, approximately 1 hour. Remove foil and bake 45 minutes more, or until top is golden brown. This bread pudding is best chilled in the refrigerator overnight then cut into squares and heated in individual portions in the microwave. If desired, create a white chocolate sauce for topping bread pudding by combining 8 ounces melted white chocolate with 3 ounces heavy whipping cream. This may be done in a double boiler or microwave.

Serves 6 to 8

APPLE FRANGIPANE TART

Recipe courtesy of Tariq Hanna from Sucre.

SHORT DOUGH

- 1 pound Plugra butter or other unsalted butter
- 1/2 pound sugar (or 1 cup plus 1 heaping tablespoon)
- 2 eggs
- 2 teaspoons vanilla extract
- 1 1/2 pounds cake flour (or 5 1/3 cups)

FRANGIPANE

- 1 stick plus 1 tablespoon butter, melted
- 10 ounces powdered sugar combined with 10 ounces almond flour
- 1/3 cup bread flour
- 5 eggs

APPLES

- 2 to 3 Fuji apples, peeled
  Cinnamon sugar

For the dough, cream butter and sugar well. Add eggs and vanilla. Add flour and mix until just blended. Refrigerate before use.

Roll out dough to 1/4-inch thickness and place in a tart mold. Trim excess dough and bake at 350 degrees for 20 minutes, or until very lightly browned.

For the frangipane, combine all ingredients until smooth.

To assemble, slice apples into 1/4-inch wedges and then sprinkle with cinnamon sugar. Fill the prebaked tart shell two-thirds with the frangipane. Arrange apples over top and bake at 350 degrees for 15 to 18 minutes. Serve warm or at room temperature.

Note: As a variation, use pears, peaches, nectarines, plums, figs, or any other firm fruit of your choice.

Serves 6 to 8

DOUGH VARIATIONS

For chocolate short dough, replace $4^{1}/_{2}$ tablespoons of flour with cocoa powder (about $2^{1}/_{2}$ ounces). For nut dough, simply add 3 ounces ground nuts of choice after flour has been added. For citrus dough, add $^{1}/_{2}$ tablespoon citrus oil of choice and 2 tablespoons zest.

FRANGIPANE VARIATIONS

For a deeper nuttier flavor, brown the butter first. Replace almond flour (finely ground almonds) with any other nut of your choice. For enhanced flavor, add $^{1}/_{4}$ cup amaretto or Frangelico.

3 Apples, by Karen Z. Haynes, courtesy Soren Christensen Gallery.

GELATO DI SESAMO, MIELE E LATTE DI CAPRA

Recipe courtesy of Carmello Truillo from La Divina.

GELATO

    4 large free-range egg yolks
1/4 teaspoon sea salt
1/2 cup evaporated cane juice
    3 cups goat milk
1/3 cup honey
1/3 cup tahini

SESAME CANDY

    2 tablespoons roasted sesame seeds
      A pinch of sea salt
    2 tablespoons honey

For the gelato, heat the egg yolks, salt, and evaporated cane juice together until pale ribbons form.

Heat the milk in a heavy-bottomed saucepan over medium heat. As the milk warms, add the honey, stirring constantly. Cook until the milk is warm. If you have a thermometer, cook the milk to 145 degrees.

Slowly pour some of the warm milk mixture into the beaten egg yolks, mixing well. Pour the yolk mixture back into the milk.

Continue to heat the milk until small bubbles rim the pan and the mixture coats the back of the spoon, being careful not to let the milk scald. If you have a thermometer, cook the milk to 185 degrees.

Mix some of the hot mixture into the tahini, then add the tahini to the hot mixutre and mix well.

Recipe continued on page 195

Tuna, by Francie Rich, courtesy Francie Rich.

Marigny Dreams, *by James Michalopoulos, courtesy Michalopoulos Gallery.*

Put the mixture in an ice bath to cool it down as much as possible, as quickly as possible. Warm milk put directly in the refrigerator will not cool down quickly enough to keep it safe.

Allow the mixture to age for at least 4 hours in the refrigerator. Gelato, like red beans and rice, tastes better the day after it is cooked.

For the candy, bring the roasted sesame seeds, a pinch of salt and honey to 280 degrees. Then spread thinly on a silicon mat and place in the freezer.

Freeze the gelato mixture in your ice cream maker according to its instructions. While the mixture is freezing, break the candy into small bits and return to the freezer. When the gelato is ready, mix in the sesame candy. You may either serve the gelato immediately, or store in your freezer for up to 3 days. Allow the gelato to sit for about 20 minutes in your refrigerator before serving if you have stored it in the freezer.

Serves 6

Sorbetto di Fragola e Balsamico

Recipe courtesy of Carmello Truillo from La Divina.

2 1/2 cups fresh Louisiana strawberries,
   or other strawberries
1 cup organic evaporated cane
   juice, divided
1 1/3 cups mineral water
3 tablespoons aged balsamic vinegar
   Freshly ground white pepper

The day before you make the sorbetto, wash the strawberries under cool running water and pat dry with paper towels. Hull them and then cut in half. Put strawberries in a bowl and cover with 1/2 cup evaporated cane juice. Mix well, cover and refrigerate overnight. The cane juice draws out the flavor of the strawberries and improves the consistency of the sorbetto without giving the strawberries a "cooked" flavor.

New Orleans from Governor Nichols Street Wharf,
by Elemore Morgan, courtesy Arthur Roger Gallery.

Bring the mineral water to a boil, add the remaining evaporated cane juice and then let boil for 2 minutes. Put the mixture in an ice bath to make it as cold as possible, as quickly as possible.

Purée the strawberries with the balsamic vinegar and mix thoroughly with the water mixture. Add about three grindings of white pepper and mix well.

Freeze the sorbetto in your ice cream maker according to directions. You can serve the sorbetto directly from the machine or you can store it in your freezer for up to three days. Let the sorbetto soften in the refrigerator for about 20 minutes before serving if you have stored it in the freezer. Garnish with sliced strawberries.

Serves 4 (yields 1 quart)

LAVENDER HONEY CRÈME CARAMEL

Recipe courtesy of Ryan Hughes from Café Degas.

Butter
1/2 cup sugar
1/2 lemon, juiced (about 2 tablespoons)
3 tablespoons water
8 egg yolks
1/4 cup honey
1/4 cup plus 2 tablespoons sugar
2 1/2 cups heavy cream
1 tablespoon dried lavender
2 teaspoons vanilla

Preheat oven to 325 degrees.

Butter ramekins. Combine sugar and lemon juice for caramel, cook until brown and then add water. Divide into ramekins.

Whip egg yolks, honey, and sugar until light ribbons form. Scald cream with lavender and vanilla and then whisk into egg mixture. Pour into ramekins and then place ramekins in a water bath. Bake, covered, for 30 minutes. Allow to cool in water bath until it reaches room temperature.

To serve, use a paring knife to release the crème from the sides of the ramekins and turn over onto individual plates.

Serves 12

Untitled Kitchens and Dining Rooms, *by Robert Brantley, courtesy Robert Brantley.*

BANANA BREAD

Recipe courtesy of Hollis Hindman Woodrow.

2	cups all-purpose flour
1/2	cup sugar
1/4	cup brown sugar
3/4	teaspoon baking soda
1/2	teaspoon salt
1/4	teaspoon cinnamon
3	ripe bananas, mashed
1/4	cup yogurt, plain or vanilla flavored
2	eggs
6	tablespoons butter, melted and cooled to room temperature
1	teaspoon rum
1/2	cup sliced or slivered almonds

Preheat oven to 350 degrees.

Butter and flour loaf pan. Whisk dry ingredients together to combine. Whisk wet ingredients together to combine. Fold wet ingredients into the dry ingredients. Pour into the prepared loaf pan and then sprinkle the almonds on top. Bake 50 to 55 minutes; cool in pan for 5 minutes and then turn onto cooling rack.

Yield 1 loaf

DIVINITY FUDGE

Recipe courtesy of Mary Ann Meyer.

4	cups sugar
1	cup water
1	cup light corn syrup
4	egg whites
1	teaspoon vanilla extract
1	cup chopped pecans

Combine sugar, water, and corn syrup and then cook to hard-ball stage (260 degrees on a candy thermometer). Beat egg whites to soft peaks and then pour hot sugar over egg whites while beating constantly. Continue to beat mixture while adding the vanilla and nuts. Pour into a buttered 9-inch-square pan and then let cool; cut into squares.

Makes 12 peices

Love Knot, by Karen Z. Haynes, *courtesy Soren Christensen Gallery.*

Dali Lama, *by Francie Rich, courtesy Francie Rich.*

ANGEL FOOD CAKE

Recipe courtesy of Elizabeth "Buzzy" McFerrin.

2 cups large egg whites (about 15 large eggs), at room temperature
1/4 teaspoon cream of tartar
1 1/2 cups granulated sugar
1 tablespoon vanilla extract
1/8 teaspoon salt
1 1/2 cups cake flour
1 1/2 cups confectioners' sugar

Using an electric mixer fitted with a wire whip, beat the egg whites on medium speed with the cream of tartar until frothy and soft peaks start to form, about 2 minutes. With the machine running, gradually add the sugar and beat until thick and opaque. Add the vanilla and salt; beat to glossy soft peaks.

Sift the flour and confectioners' sugar into the egg white mixture, folding gently to incorporate. Gently pour the batter into an ungreased 10-inch tube pan or a 10-inch-round cake pan and bake until the top forms a light brown crust and pulls away from the sides, about 40 to 45 minutes.

Invert the cake immediately onto a cooling rack and let cool completely. Cut between the edge of the cake and the pan with a long thin knife and slowly remove the cake from the pan.

Use a serrated knife to cut the cake into individual slices and serve. The cake will keep for 2 to 3 days at room temperature.

Makes 1 (10-inch) cake

BUTTERMILK BISCUIT STRAWBERRY SHORTCAKE WITH SWEETENED WHIPPED CREAM

Recipe courtesy of Elizabeth "Buzzy" McFerrin.

3 pints fresh strawberries, rinsed clean, tops trimmed, and quartered
1 cup granulated sugar
1/4 cup amaretto or other almond-flavored liqueur
1 quart cold heavy cream
1/4 cup confectioners' sugar, plus more for garnish
1 teaspoon pure vanilla extract
Buttermilk Biscuits (see below)
Sliced almonds, lightly toasted, for garnish

BUTTERMILK BISCUITS

4 cups all-purpose flour
2 tablespoons baking powder
3/4 cup granulated sugar
1 teaspooon baking soda
1 teaspooon salt
1/2 cup cold unsalted butter, cut into small cubes
1/2 cup Crisco or other solid vegetable shortening
2 cups buttermilk

Combine the strawberries, granulated sugar, and amaretto in a large bowl and toss to combine. Let stand at room temperature for at least 20 minutes and up to 24 hours, gently stirring occasionally, until the sugar is dissolved. Refrigerate, covered, until ready to assemble the desserts.

Combine the heavy cream with the confectioners' sugar in a large bowl and beat with an electric mixer or whisk until slightly thickened. Add the vanilla and continue to beat until the mixture forms soft peaks.

When ready to assemble the desserts, split the biscuits in half crosswise and place the bottom halves on dessert plates. Spoon the strawberry mixture onto the biscuits and top with a large dollop of sweetened whipped cream. Arrange the biscuit tops on an angle over the strawberries and cream and then sprinkle each serving with additional confectioners' sugar. Garnish the top of each serving with sliced almonds and serve immediately.

For the biscuits, preheat the oven to 400 degrees. Line a large baking sheet with parchment paper and set aside.

Combine the flour, baking powder, sugar, baking soda, and salt in a large bowl. Add the butter and Crisco and work it in with your fingers or a fork until the mixture resembles coarse crumbs. Add the buttermilk and mix it with your fingers just until the dough comes together and the dry ingredients are wet, being very careful not to overwork the dough.

Lightly dust a work surface with flour. Turn the dough out onto the work surface and pat into a $^3/_4$- to 1-inch-thick round. Cut out the biscuits with a 3-inch cookie cutter, gathering and re-rolling the scraps. Place the biscuits about 1-inch apart on the prepared baking sheet and bake until golden brown, about 12 to 15 minutes.

Cool the biscuits on a wire rack to serve as Strawberry Shortcakes, or serve as desired.

Note: Biscuits may be frozen on baking sheets and kept for several weeks. This recipe is very adaptable and all component recipes can easily be halved. Also, use whatever fruit is in season.

Variation: To make savory biscuits, reduce the sugar from $^3/_4$ cup to 2 tablespoons, or leave it out entirely.

Serves 10 to 12

COCONUT BREAD PUDDING WITH CARAMEL SAUCE

Recipe courtesy of Elizabeth "Buzzy" McFerrin.

1 1/2 long loaves French bread (2 1/2 to 3 feet in length), cut into 1-inch cubes
1 (13.5-ounce) can coconut milk
1 cup shredded coconut
15 large eggs
6 cups heavy cream
3 cups sugar
Caramel Sauce (see below)

CARAMEL SAUCE
2 cups sugar
1 tablespoon water
1 tablespoon fresh lemon juice
1 cup heavy cream

Preheat the oven to 350 degrees.

Place the bread cubes in a 9 x 13-inch baking dish and top with the coconut milk and coconut. Beat the eggs in a large bowl.

Combine the cream and sugar in a medium saucepan over medium heat and cook, stirring occasionally, until the sugar is dissolved. Slowly whisk the cream mixture into the eggs to combine. Pour the egg mixture over the bread and let soak for 5 to 10 minutes. Mix together the bread and egg mixture with your hands, squeezing the bread cubes so the mixture is absorbed. Cover the dish with aluminum foil and bake until set, about 1 hour.

Uncover and continue cooking until the top is golden brown, about 15 to 20 minutes more; let cool for 10 minutes. To serve, spoon the bread pudding onto plates and drizzle each serving with Caramel Sauce.

For the sauce, combine the sugar, water, and lemon juice in a heavy saucepan and cook over medium-high heat, stirring until the sugar dissolves. Let the mixture boil without stirring until it turns a deep amber color, about 2 to 3 minutes, and remove it from the heat if it starts to burn. Add the cream carefully (it will bubble up), whisk to combine, and remove from the heat. Let cool to just warm before serving. (The sauce will thicken as it cools.)

Note: It's important to use coconut milk in this recipe, not a sweetened product like Coco Lopez.

Also, bread puddings are ideal for parties since they can be made ahead of time up to the point of baking and then refrigerated overnight. Bring the pudding to room temperature before baking, or increase the cooking time by about 20 minutes.

Serves 12

Peek-A-Boo, *by Michael Marlowe, courtesy Soren Christensen Gallery.*

Pastries, *by Amy McKinnon, courtesy Amy McKinnon.*

Gateau de Sirop (Syrup Cake)

Recipe courtesy of Ken Smith.

1/2	cup vegetable oil
1 1/2	cups Steen's Syrup*
1	egg, beaten
2 1/2	cups sifted flour
1	teaspoon cinnamon
1	teaspoon ginger
1/4	teaspoon cloves
1/2	teaspoon salt
1 1/2	teaspoons baking soda
3/4	cup hot water

* Can be purchased online.

Preheat oven to 350 degrees.

Grease and flour an 8-inch-round pan.

Combine oil, syrup, and egg; stir until well blended. Mix and resift all dry ingredients except baking soda. Add dry ingredients to the oil mixture alternately with the hot water in which the baking soda has been dissolved. Begin and end with flour mixture. Pour into prepared pan and then bake 45 minutes. Cool in pan on a wire rack.

Serves 6

RESOURCES

Chef Scott Snodgrass
One Restaurant & Lounge
8132 Hampson St
New Orleans, LA 70118
(504) 301-9061
www.one-sl.com

Chef Tom Wolfe
Peristyle
1041 Dumaine St
New Orleans, LA 70116
(504) 593-9535
peristylerestaurant.com

Chef Chuck Subra
La Cote Brasserie
700 Tchoupitoulas St
New Orleans, LA 70130
(504) 613-2350
www.lacotebrasserie.com

Chef Brian Landry
Galatoire's Restaurant Inc
209 Bourbon St
New Orleans, LA 70130
(504) 525-2021
www.galatoires.com

Chef Matt Guidry
Meauxbar
942 N Rampart St
New Orleans, LA 70116
(504) 569-9979
www.meauxbar.com

Chef Bob Iacavone
Cuvee Restaurant
322 Magazine St
New Orleans, LA 70130
(504) 587-9001
www.restaurantcuvee.com

Chef Stephen G. Schwarz
Mat and Naddies
937 Leonidas St
New Orleans, LA 70118
(504) 861-9600
www.matandnaddies.com

Chef Greg Sonnier
Gabrielle's
Goodeats5673@aol.com

Chef Emanuelle Loubier
Dante's Kitchen
736 Dante St
New Orleans, LA 70118
(504) 861-3121
www.danteskitchen.com

Chef Ryan Hughes
Cafe Degas
3127 Esplanade Ave
New Orleans, LA 70119
(504) 945-5635
www.cafedegas.com

Chef Greg Picolo
The Bistro At Maison de Ville
727 Rue Toulouse
New Orleans, LA 70130
(504)528-9206
www.hotelmaisondeville.com/dining/

Chefs Rich and Danielle Sutton
The St. James Cheese Company
5004 Prytania St
New Orleans, LA 70118
(504) 899-4737
www.stjamescheese.com

Chef Adolfo Garcia
Rio Mar Restaurant
800 S Peters St
New Orleans, LA 70130
(504) 525-3474
www.riomarseafood.com

Chef Jack Leonardi
Jacques-Imo's Cafe
8324 Oak St
New Orleans, LA 70118
(504) 861-0886
jacquesimoscafe.com

Chef Donald Link
Herbsaint
701 Saint Charles Ave
New Orleans, LA 70130
(504) 524-4114
www.herbsaint.com

Cochon
930 Tchoupitoulas St
New Orleans, LA 70130
(504) 588-2123
www.cochonrestaurant.com

Poppy Tooker
Savvy Gourmet
4519 Magazine St
New Orleans, LA 70115
(504) 895-2665
www.savvygourmet.com

Slow Food New Orleans
Convivium lead by Poppy Tooker
and the Savvy Gourmet

Chef Tariq Hanna
Sucre
3025 Magazine St
New Orleans, LA 70115
(504) 520-8311
www.shopsucre.com

Chef/Owners Carmello
    and Katrina Turillo
La Divina Gelateria LLC
3005 Magazine St
New Orleans, LA 70115
(504) 342-2634
www.ladivinagelateria.com

Chef John Folse & Company
2517 S. Philippe Ave
Gonzales, LA 70737
(225) 644-6000
www.jfolse.com

Chef Corbin Evans
(504) 782-7836
www.chefcorbin.com
Private dinners, in-home classes,
personal chef

Chef Ken Smith
chefkenneth@bellsouth.net

Chef Kevin Vizard
Vizard's
2203 Saint Charles Ave
New Orleans, LA 70130
(505) 529-9912
www.vizardsontheavenue.com

MUSEUMS, GALLERIES,
AND ARTISTS

Ogden Museum of Southern Art,
    University of New Orleans
925 Camp St
New Orleans, LA 70130
(504) 539-9600
www.ogdenmuseum.org

The Historic New Orleans Collection
533 Royal St
New Orleans, LA 70130
(504) 523-4662
www.hnoc.org

New Orleans Museum of Art
One Collins Diboll Circle, City Park
New Orleans, LA 70124
(504) 658-4100
www.noma.org

Contemporary Arts Center
900 Camp St
New Orleans, LA 70130
(504) 528-3805
www.cacno.org

The Newcomb Art Gallery
Woldenberg Art Center
Tulane University
New Orleans, LA 70118
(504) 865-5328
newcomb.tulane.edu/artindex.html

Southern Food and
    Beverage Museum
1 Poydras St #169
New Orleans, LA 70130
(504) 539-9617
www.southernfood.org

Soren Christensen Gallery
400 Julia St
New Orleans, LA 70130
(504) 569-9501
www.sorengallery.com

Bryant Galleries of New Orleans
316 Royal St
New Orleans, LA 70130
(504) 525-5584 or (800) 844-1994
www.bryantgalleries.com

Cole Pratt Gallery
3800 Magazine St
New Orleans, LA 70115
(504) 891-6789
www.coleprattgallery.com

Carol Robinson Gallery
840 Napoleon Ave
New Orleans, LA 70115
(504) 895-6130
www.carolrobinsongallery.com

Anton Haardt Gallery
2858 Magazine St
New Orleans, LA 70115
(504) 891-9080
www.antonart.com

Rolland Golden
Lucille Golden
(504) 615-1822
www.rollandgolden.com

Fredrick Guess Studio
910 Royal St
New Orleans, Louisiana 70116
(504) 581-4596
(504) 999-9999 (fax)
info@fredrickguessstudio.com

Arthur Roger Gallery
432 Julia St
New Orleans, LA 70130
(504) 522-1999
www.arthurrogergallery.com

A.G. Wagner Studio and Gallery
813 Royal St
New Orleans, La 70130
(504) 561-7440

Jason Langley
www.seekingfocus.com
www.reciprocityimages.com

LeMieux Galleries
Denise R. Berthiaume
332 Julia St
New Orleans, LA 70130
(504) 522-5988
www.lemieuxgalleries.com
denise@lemieuxgalleries.com

Amy McKinnon
www.habitualpainter.com

James Michalopoulos
617 Bienville St
New Orleans, LA 70130
(504) 558-0505
www.michalopoulos.com

John Preble
UCM Museum
22275 Hwy 36
Abita Springs, LA 70420
(985) 892-2624
www.ucmmuseum.com

Robert Brantley
Brantley and Brantley
2624 S. Carrollton Ave
New Orleans, La 70118

The Dusti Bonge Foundation
Julian Brunt
P.O. Box 1425
Biloxi, Ms 39533

Realizations
Walter Anderson
1000 Washington Ave
Ocean Springs, MS 39564
(228) 875-0503

Blue Spiral Gallery
38 Biltmore Ave
Asheville, NC 28804
(828) 251-0202

INGREDIENTS

Steen's Cane Syrup
P.O. Box 339
119 N. Main St
Abbeville, LA 70510
(800) 725-1654
steens@steenssyrup.com

Community Coffee
Community Coffee Company
P.O. Box 2311
Baton Rouge, LA 70821
(800) 525-5583
Fax: (800) 643-8199
www.communitycoffee.com
ccc@communitycoffee.com

Café du Monde
(800)772-2927
www.cafedumonde.com
Beignet mix

Creole Country
512 David St
New Orleans, LA 70119-4711
(504) 488-1263
Fax: (504) 488-4810
Andouille sausage

Kalustyan's
Marhaba International Inc.
123 Lexington Ave
New York, NY 10016
(800) 352-3451
www.kalustyans.com
Spices, Asian and Indian ingredients

Sunrise Asian Food Market
70 West 29th Ave
Eugene, OR 97405
(541) 343-3295
www.sunriseasianfood.com

INDEX

METRIC CONVERSION CHART

Volume Measurements		Weight Measurements		Temperature Measurements	
U.S.	Metric	U.S.	Metric	U.S.	Metric
1 teaspoon	5 ml	1/2 ounce	15 g	250	120
1 tablespoon	15 ml	1 ounce	30 g	300	150
1/4 cup	60 ml	3 ounces	90 g	325	160
1/3 cup	75 ml	4 ounces	115 g	350	180
1/2 cup	125 ml	8 ounces	225 g	375	190
2/3 cup	150 ml	12 ounces	350 g	400	200
3/4 cup	175 ml	1 pound	450 g	425	220
1 cup	250 ml	2 1/4 pounds	1 kg	450	230